DOMINICK ALBANO

The
Fundamental

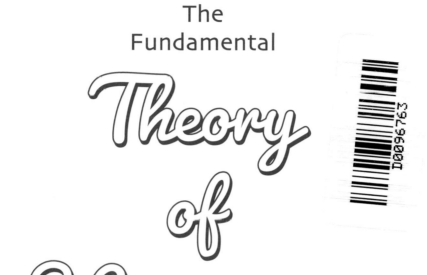

Theory
of
Happiness

How to find your purpose and be more joyful

ASCENSION

West Chester, Pennsylvania

For Rebecca—

I'm never really happy without you.

Ascension
PO Box 1990
West Chester, PA 19380
1-800-376-0520
ascensionpress.com

Cover design: Kathleen Raymundo

Printed in the United States of America
ISBN 978-1-950784-10-3

CONTENTS

Let's Begin

"Mom, this is Welles. I want you to know that I'm OK."

—9:12AM, SEPTEMBER 11, 2001

Welles Remy Crowther grew up in the quiet suburb of Nyack, New York. He loved sports and school, doted upon his younger sisters, and looked up to his father and mother.

As Welles grew, so did his character. His personality was magnetic. He was known for being kind and generous, for always thinking of others before himself, and for his signature red bandanna, which his father gave him one Sunday before church when he was six. From that day on, he always had that red bandanna tucked in his back pocket or underneath his helmet during lacrosse games. The day he turned sixteen, he became a volunteer firefighter.

After graduating from Boston College, Welles took a prestigious job as an equities trader in New York City. Welles had everything the world told him he needed to be happy: loving family, good friends, a lucrative career. But there was a problem. He wasn't happy. Not really. At some point Welles realized there had to be more to life than his career and his accomplishments. He needed to find who he really was and what he was made to do.

Welles called his dad with surprising news: He wanted to change careers. He felt unfulfilled behind his desk. It wasn't what he was meant to do. He didn't feel like the person he was meant to be. He told his dad that he wanted to help people—

that he wanted to be a New York City firefighter. He knew he only had one life to live, only one chance to find his true purpose.

On September 11, 2001, Welles lived out that purpose. The meaning of his life.

Welles was at his desk on the 104th floor of the World Trade Center South Tower when American Airlines Flight 11 struck the North Tower at 8:46 AM.

Sixteen minutes later, United Airlines Flight 175 struck the South Tower.

At 9:12 AM, minutes after the plane hit the South Tower, Welles called his mom and left a voicemail: "Mom, this is Welles. I want you to know that I'm OK."

As Welles' father stood in his living room and watched the South Tower fall, he fell to his knees and prayed to God through his tears, "Dear God. Take me now. Leave him here. Take me now. Leave him here." To his father, Welles was more than a son. He was his best friend.

When his mother heard that the tower had fallen, she knew. She knew the way only a mother could. She knew her son was gone.

Welles' body was found in the lobby of the South Tower on March 19, 2002.

Months later, the *New York Times* printed stories of survivors from inside the South Tower. Welles' mother was reading these stories when a detail—a detail that would mean nothing to the rest of the world—struck her. One woman told the story of a bold young man who led her to safety. A bold young man wearing a red bandanna.

"Welles," his mother said, "I found you."

Welles' mother began reaching out to survivors from the South Tower to discover the last moments of her beloved son's life.

When the plane struck the tower between the seventy-eighth and eighty-fourth floors, around two hundred people were in the seventy-eighth-floor lobby waiting by the elevators to evacuate the building. The explosion rocked the room, injuring or killing everyone in its path. The smoke and blood and bodies made the room unrecognizable. Those who survived were disoriented from being thrown across the room. Many thought the floor might collapse underneath them if they moved.

Then a man burst on the scene. He cried out that he had found the stairwell and that anyone who could stand should follow him to safety.

He carried a woman over his shoulder while leading survivors down sixteen flights of stairs to where the air was clear. He set down the woman he was carrying, told the group to keep going, and ran back up to the seventy-eighth-floor lobby.

He began putting out fires, administering first aid to survivors, and helping those who were too disoriented to help themselves.

Then he cried out, "Everyone who can stand, stand now. If you can help others, do so," and led a second group to the open stairwell. Once they were safely on their way, he turned around and ran back into the sky lobby.

Witnesses say the man brought at least twelve people to safety that day. One of the survivors reported, "If he hadn't come back, I wouldn't have made it. People can live one hundred years and not have the compassion, the wherewithal to do what he did."

Though none of the survivors knew who he was, none of them could forget his heroic efforts, or the red bandanna he had wrapped around his nose and mouth to protect himself from the smoke. The signature red bandanna of Welles Remy Crowther.

In 2006, Welles was posthumously named a New York City firefighter in a ceremony attended by his family as well as one of the survivors that he rescued that day and her family.

Welles called his dad telling him he wanted to change careers because he didn't know who he was or what he was meant to do with his life. Because of that, he wasn't happy.

But for fifty-seven minutes on September 11, 2001, Welles Remy Crowther, in the most horrific of circumstances, clearly knew exactly who he was and exactly what he was made to do. He gave his life to be that person. He lived more fully alive in those minutes than many do in a lifetime.

Part I:
Something to Live For

MORE THAN FINE

"Once you realize how good you really are, you never settle for playing less than your best."
REGGIE JACKSON

"How are you doing?"

It's a question we ask a dozen times a day, and the answer is always the same.

Most people respond with "good" or "fine" or some other cliché. Why? Maybe we don't think the person asking really cares. Maybe we don't really care to share the truth. Maybe we don't even know the truth.

We see this interaction a hundred times a week. Whether the person asking doesn't really want to know or the person answering doesn't tell the truth, nothing makes life and relationships seem more superficial than this surface-level interaction.

For me, the question is too hard to answer. My life is filled with blessings, opportunities, and treasures, but also challenges, stress, and suffering—and everything in between.

I've thought a lot about this question over the past year, and the truth is, how I'm doing doesn't particularly depend on all that anymore. How I'm doing isn't dependent on life's balance sheet—blessings versus hardships, joy versus suffering. I've discovered a completely different way to live that doesn't depend on all that, and explaining the journey that got me to this point takes a lot more time than simply responding to a passing question from a casual interaction.

But I'm going to tell you the whole story. It involves a set of steps and guidelines that I call the Fundamental Theory of Happiness.

THE PURSUIT OF MORE

"We know what we are, but know not what we may be."
WILLIAM SHAKESPEARE

How is it that we can have all the riches and fame and fortune and success in the world, and still be unfulfilled and unhappy? You've seen people living like this. The public figures, the celebrities, the business leaders. You may even know some of them.

How is it that we can have next to nothing in the eyes of the world and exude a contagious joy? You've seen these joyous people and know them too. But so many more of them go unnamed. From the local serviceman or -woman to your grandmother.

Why is it that we can go to third-world communities to serve the poor and the sick and find more joy in the hearts of the people there than the people we call neighbors back home?

One group is living the Fundamental Theory of Happiness, and one isn't. I'll bet you can guess which is which.

To explain, let me take you back to before I discovered the Fundamental Theory of Happiness …

My head fell back into the passenger seat as I watched the golden glow of the lights along the highway flick by, one after the other. My eyes lost focus, and soon my mind began to wander.

My thoughts drifted from the work we had done that night, to the organization I was running, to my wife and children, who would be asleep by the time I was home.

I was still staring out the window a few minutes later when I asked my friend, "Is this all there is to life?"

"What do you mean?"

A deep rush escaped my lips as I thought about what words would make him understand.

"I'm twenty-eight years old, and I've got everything the world says I should want. Everything that's supposed to make me happy. I'm married to the girl of my dreams, I adore my two kids, and I founded an organization with my best friends that's having a monumental impact in the community. I've got great friends and a house and a dog and two cars. We go on vacation and spend holidays with the family. But I keep wondering, what's next?"

"If I have everything the world tells me I should want and I'm doing everything I'm supposed to do, why don't I feel the way they—whoever they are—say I'm supposed to feel? I'm supposed to be living the dream. I'm supposed to feel full and complete and happy. But instead I feel like I need to have and achieve more. Like what I have now isn't … enough."

He didn't know how to respond, and I didn't blame him. It's not that I was unhappy. I wasn't sad or depressed, but my life had become a hamster wheel, and no matter how hard or fast I ran, I felt like I wasn't getting anywhere. When was enough finally going to feel like enough?

I had lived my life up to this point according to certain unwritten rules I had picked up over the years. They didn't come intentionally. I wasn't groomed for them. No one taught me these rules in a systematic way. They were taught to me by my experiences, by my relationships, by my successes and failures, by my desires, by my teachers, by pain, and by everything else that contributes to this thing we call life.

If I had to codify the rules governing my life at this point, they'd be (in no particular order)

- Achieve something great.

- Be a good person.

- Have fun.

- Fulfill your spiritual obligations.

- Have nice things.

- Be adventurous.

- Be responsible.

- Have as many great experiences as you can.

- Be a great dad and husband.

- Carpe diem!

It's not a bad list. I'm sure you can imagine (or even know) someone who seems to live life guided by a much worse set of principles. The problem was where the rules were getting me.

These rules had brought me a pretty great life. I had made it to the top—metaphorically. I might not have had the corner office, but I had a beautiful wife I loved deeply. I had two sons who were my greatest source of pure joy on this planet. I had a great job and positive career trajectory. I loved my job, and my work was meaningful. We weren't rich, but we had enough to own a decent house and two cars. We spent holidays with family and vacationed in the summers. Our faith was important to us. We went to church every Sunday and prayed often.

But the rules also made me feel like I needed more. My marriage needed to look more like a fairy tale. My kids needed to be perfect. I needed to achieve more at work. I needed more money, a nicer house, and nicer cars. I needed more vacation time in more exotic locations. Our holidays needed to be filled with more memories and nostalgia and traditions. I needed to do great deeds that people would notice. I needed to live a faith that people admired.

I was living in the **pursuit of more**. I asked the question, "Is this all there is to life?" But what I really wanted to know was, "Is there something better to live for?"

This is the question that has driven me. It's rattled me. It's caused me to question everything. It led me to write this book.

ONE SIMPLE QUESTION

"Most folks are about as happy as they make up their minds to be."

ABRAHAM LINCOLN

Your journey toward being Fundamentally Happy starts with a simple question:

What do you want?

Simple, because the entirety of the answer is inside of you. It doesn't require advanced degrees or deep philosophical insight to be able to answer it. And yet, as simple as the question is, it is also profound and, sometimes, very difficult to answer.

It all comes down to context. If we're prepping for dinner and my wife asks me what I want, the answer is easy: a burrito. If my boss asks me what I want from my career, it gets a bit more complicated. If a friend asks what I want out of life, it gets more complicated still.

I want to know what you really want out of life. But that's a difficult question to answer. So let me propose a more fundamental way of understanding it:

Do you want to spend your life pursuing more, or do you want to live for something better?

The Fundamental Theory of Happiness is about getting out of your own way and designing a life for something better.

LIVING THE DREAM

"The greater part of our happiness or misery depends on our dispositions, and not on our circumstances. We carry the seeds of the one or the other about with us in our minds wherever we go."

MARTHA WASHINGTON

It had all the makings of a miserable day, but I couldn't keep the smile off my face.

It all started the night before. The thunderous sound of stampeding toddler feet was the first thing to greet me as I opened the door. The little boys went nearly airborne as they slammed into me, squeezing my neck until it hurt. My wife took my bag and travel mug as she placed a delicate kiss on my cheek, and my oldest son's voice drifted in lazily from the living room, "Hey, Dad."

You could see just how green the grass was turning in the glow of the spring sun. A light breeze of warm air came in through the screen door, and we decided to have dinner outside. I guarded the hot dogs on the grill while my wife brought out platters of watermelon and corn on the cob. I couldn't decide if my boys were disgusting or adorable as the watermelon juice and butter from the corn on the cob dripped from their chins.

I knew just what we needed. I darted into the garage and dug out the Whiffle Ball bat and some bases, and as a family we played an epic game in the backyard. The boys beat me—but only because I let them.

The boys carried in the plates as I did the dishes, we helped the little guys get on their pj's and brush their teeth, I lay in bed with them and read some books, we knelt by the bed and said our prayers, and then it was lights out. It was hard to keep my eyes open once the house was quiet.

Then the storms rolled in. The crackle of thunder and the howling of cold wind came like spring wanted to remind us just how quickly everything could change. Soon scared little feet were scurrying into our bed, and sleep became much more difficult with little knees and elbows sticking into my back and sides all night.

It was still dark when my alarm went off. I felt like lead lying there, but my body hurt from the awkward angles, so I got up quick enough. I got into work early, like I always do. I like being there when it's still dark and quiet.

I was just settling into the office when my cell phone buzzed on my desk. It was my best friend. My face fell as I heard him explain that we had to cancel our long-planned camping trip.

By the time I hung up the phone, I felt like it was time for my great source of comfort and strength: coffee. I snatched the empty mug off my desk and made my way across the empty office to the break room. On my way back, full mug of fresh coffee in hand, I ran into a coworker who had also gotten in early. She asked how my night had gone.

"Great!" I told her, and then I filled her in on all the details of grilling out and Whiffle Ball with the family.

She smiled. "You are living my dream."

I sat back down at my desk, thinking about how this could have been the start to a miserable day. Nothing dramatic had happened. No one had died. I hadn't found out I had cancer. I didn't lose my job. But the lack of sleep, the canceled plans, and the weather were enough to set most days on a course that you couldn't recover from.

The world looked uninviting and cold, I had disappointments to deal with, and I felt tired.

But this wasn't going to be a miserable day. I smiled. I was living the dream.

And I never would've felt that way if I hadn't discovered a new way to think about happiness.

A THEORY OF HAPPINESS?

"We either make ourselves miserable, or we make ourselves happy. The amount of work is the same."

CARLOS CASTANEDA

The dictionary defines "theory" in a couple of different ways:

1. A plausible or scientifically acceptable general principle or body of principles offered to explain phenomena.

Examples of this kind of theory would be Einstein's theory of relativity or the big bang theory. With this kind of theory, you can typically expect to have a statement or law with evidence to support and back up the theory.

But there is another way to define "theory" according to your average dictionary:

2. The general principles or rules that aid in the practice of an art, activity, or science.

Examples of this kind of theory would be music theory, art theory, or productivity theory.

While most of us can pass through life without giving much thought to Einstein's theory of relativity, the truth is that all of us encounter theories of this second kind every single day.

There is a theory to how to drive a car. We learn the general principles or rules of driving that help us practice that activity. There is a theory to how you do your work. Whatever your profession, there are general principles and rules you follow that help you be successful. There is a theory to just about everything you do.

You want to run a marathon, so what do you do? You go out and buy a book with a training regimen that teaches you the general principles or rules that aid in the practice of running a marathon. That's the theory of running a marathon.

You want to write a book? You go out and buy books on writing that teach you the general principles or guiding rules that help you write a book. That's writing theory.

Theory is all around us.

The Fundamental Theory of Happiness is not the first definition of theory. It is not a grand idea with a single statement or law. Happiness is not a phenomenon. A2 + B2 will never equal "happiness." Science cannot make you happy.

The Fundamental Theory of Happiness comes from three main sources.

The first is the Fundamentally Happy themselves. The Fundamentally Happy are all around us. You probably know some of them. They are not defined by what they do or what they have. Their happiness is not dependent on another person, possession, or position. They are unaffected by the weather, luck, the person in the car next to them, or any other exterior factors. They are driven by something deeper. I've met millionaires who are the Fundamentally Happy, and I've met the Fundamentally Happy living on the streets. When you meet the Fundamentally Happy, you feel invigorated and energetic.

You can contrast them with the fundamentally unhappy. You know these people too. They are driven by possessions, power, and praise. The world around them controls their mood and outlook. They drain your energy. Anything can set them off. When you leave them, you feel worse about yourself and the world.

I've observed the Fundamentally Happy. I've studied them. I've interviewed them. I've been mentored by them. The Fundamental Theory of Happiness shares the wisdom of the happiest people I know.

The second source is my own life experience. I've struggled with happiness. I've wondered about happiness on the deepest levels. But I've also spent my life working with people. I've led retreats. I've given talks to tens of thousands. I've served as a minister in churches and schools. I've spent an hour with thousands of people and a thousand hours walking with just one person. I've heard a thousand stories and carried the burdens of a thousand different souls.

Experience can be a brutal teacher. Sometimes we don't learn experience's lesson until days or months or years later. It's hard to enter into our sufferings and learn from them, but the wise go there.

The last source I drew from for this book is the wisdom from the greatest lessons taught by the greatest teachers in history. Only the fool ignores the wise, and while our culture has become obsessed with the new and the young, the ancient still contain truths relevant to us today. Ben Franklin, Aristotle, Mother Teresa, Plato, Joan of Arc, Soren Kierkegaard, Jesus Christ. They might not get headlines today, but they offer the collective wisdom of tens of thousands of men and women to anyone who is willing to listen.

This book will break down the general principles and rules of the Fundamental Theory of Happiness so you can implement it in your own life. Each part of this book corresponds to one of the five steps that will help you discover true happiness for yourself.

The Fundamental Theory of Happiness must be discovered. You can't learn it. These rules are already written deep on your heart and your soul. You just have to uncover the truth. The steps and strategies in this book can be used with incredible results—but only if you pursue them with vigor. Your life will only change if you get up and start doing.

The steps of the Fundamental Theory of Happiness are

1. **Become Dissatisfied.** Through life, we all gather rules that stand in the way of our happiness. We will begin by examining these false philosophies so we can be free from their influence. When we

cast aside these false philosophies, we become free to know ourselves and to be known by others. We will examine how to cope with not always doing what we want to do and sometimes doing exactly what we do not want to do.

2. **A Deeper Perception.** This step is about learning just how much our perspective on ourselves and the world around us matters. We will learn the five levels of perception and how to use silence and solitude to see and sense what is going on in our lives. We will see what the clock on the wall can teach us about who we are and what we are meant to do.

3. **Face Your Enemies.** If you want to defeat someone in battle, the greatest strategy you can implement is convincing your opponent that you do not exist. In this chapter, we will examine four enemies of happiness, what they do, how they do it, and how to overcome them.

4. **The Permanent Principle.** In this step, we figure out our purpose. No philosophy or head games here. The goal is to get clear about who we are, how others see us, and how we relate to the world.

5. **The Elusive Art of Being.** This step is all about taking the power of our identity and letting it flow into our actions. The Fundamental Theory of Happiness is useless if we can't live it. We will discuss how to orient and assemble our daily life so our actions flow from our identity to fulfill our purpose. No more wasted time.

Last note: This book is not meant to be read. Seriously. This book is meant to be *lived*.

Mark it up! Underline and highlight. Tear out pages and stick them on your bathroom mirror. Snap pictures with your phone of the ideas and challenges you want to implement in your daily life. Keep a journal nearby to help you process what you're reading.

Seriously, don't just read this book. You'll get nothing out of it. But if you read it and apply the ideas to your life with any amount of vigor, I promise things will dramatically change. They did for me.

To help you live the book, there are some helpful nuggets spread throughout that you'll encounter as you go along.

Neuroscience

My lovely wife Rebecca—who happens to have her Ph.D. in neuroscience—graciously helped me with the scientific research behind this book, and we've included some of her favorite asides to help flesh out how the ideas in the book relate to what's actually happening neurologically in our search for happiness.

Hey, are you with me?

I had a brief stint as a high school teacher, so I'm prone to repeating myself to get a point across (and I'm not above playfully throwing a piece of chalk at you if I think you're falling asleep). Think of these sections as a little pellet of chalk flying off the page to make sure that you're awake, that you're understanding what we're talking about, and that you haven't been lulled into that space where you are reading and not comprehending.

A Fundamental Truth

Truth bombs. That's what these are. They are bolded. They are typically short. They are the key ideas that the Fundamental Theory of Happiness is built on. If all you did was memorize these truths and live your life according to them, you'd have a happiness that surpasses understanding.

Theory in Practice

These TIPS (clever, eh?) are to help you actually put the ideas of the book into action. Ideas, if not put into action, are basically useless. These TIPS are there to give you concrete and specific ideas of how to implement the ideas of the book in your daily life.

Think of this book as a headlamp and a map. There is (metaphorical) gold to be found in the hills of this thing we call life. There are golden veins of happiness deep in your heart and soul and in the world around you. I just want to give you a headlamp and a map to make it a bit easier to find that happiness.

Neuroscience

THE HAPPY BRAIN

What does happiness look like in the brain? Is there a specific formula for it? Science has found that there are four main chemicals responsible for making you feel happy. The first chemical is the neurotransmitter dopamine. Dopamine plays a large role in motivation and reward. It is released when anticipating a reward. This is what motivates you to accomplish a goal. Then, once your goal is accomplished, more dopamine is released, rewarding you for a job well done by making you feel energized and happy.

The next chemical is the hormone oxytocin. Often called the "cuddle hormone," oxytocin is released during skin-to-skin contact. It is responsible for feeling close to others and bonding. It is released, for example, when holding hands, or when a mother nurses her baby. Oxytocin is also responsible for building social relationships and trust. It is released when you make eye contact and are attentive to other people.

The third chemical in the "formula" of happiness is the neurotransmitter serotonin. Serotonin is produced both in the brain and in the gut. It is responsible for regulating our mood. Serotonin is released when you feel valued or important or even when you remember a time you felt important or successful. People with high levels of serotonin are often described as being happy and have greater self-esteem. People diagnosed with depression often have lower levels of serotonin.

Last, but not least, are endorphins. Endorphins, meaning "endogenous morphine," are produced by your nervous system in response to pain in order to mask the pain or discomfort. They are what cause "runner's high," a runner's ability to push past the discomfort and keep running. They help you persevere through physically difficult tasks.

Need a boost of happiness? Now that you know more about the chemicals in your brain that make you feel happy, you can use them to help boost your happiness. Try setting small goals and rewarding yourself when you achieve them to get that release of dopamine. To boost your mood, remember a time when you felt important or successful; this will release serotonin. Need a boost of oxytocin? One of the quickest ways is to give a hug. But you can also get out from behind the computer and connect with people face-to-face. And you will be happy to know you don't have to go for a run to release endorphins. Endorphins are also released when you stretch or laugh, or even when you eat chocolate.

Part II:
How to Become
Fundamentally Happy

Step I:
Become Dissatisfied

LIFTING THE FILTER

*"All that is gold does not glitter,
not all those who wander are lost."*
J.R.R. TOLKIEN

I stared down at the coffee mug on the table, slowly running my finger around the smooth ceramic.

Could I tell them? Should I tell them?

We sat at the same scuffed table as always. We still had the watery eyes and disheveled hair that came with getting up too early. We'd been meeting at this coffee shop every Thursday morning at 5:30 for more than a year.

We met to talk about life and to share and support one another. Sometimes we gave advice, sometimes we talked things through, sometimes we helped each other, and sometimes we just laughed. Four best friends doing life together.

But could I really tell them about this?

I woke up that morning feeling like I was always feeling these days: empty.

I didn't want to see my friends. I didn't want to drink coffee or eat pastries.

I traced the ceramic rim of the coffee mug and wondered what they would think if they knew the real me. I wondered what would happen if I let them in. Would they think I was messed up? Would I freak them out?

At this point, I wasn't sure I cared enough to worry. That was the problem. I didn't care anymore.

Food didn't taste good. It was fuel. No matter what I ate, I'd just be hungry again.

Music stopped being music. It was just noise.

I didn't care about the baseball game. There was just going to be another one tomorrow no matter who won or lost tonight.

I didn't want to watch movies or TV. They were just the same old stories masquerading behind bigger bangs and more lights.

I just didn't care anymore.

Sometimes I'd sit in my car in silence and stare off into space. I wouldn't move or think or do … anything. What was the point?

Only two parts of my life brought me any sort of peace or joy: my time with my wife and kids and my time in prayer. But even then, I was quieter. Less animated. My wife knew something was wrong, and she wanted to help, but I couldn't explain things properly.

How do you tell someone you love, who wants you to be happy, who is the best thing in your life, that you aren't happy, and you don't think there is anything they can do about it?

I looked up from the mug and let my head hang in a permanent shrug. I raised the mug to my lips and tried to let the coffee burn away all these thoughts, but they weren't going anywhere.

No, I thought, *I won't talk to them about this today. I don't know what to tell them because I don't understand it myself. But that has to change. Something's not right, and I need to figure it out.*

This was the beginning. The first step toward discovering the better life I was looking for. The first step to living the Fundamental Theory of Happiness.

The first step is to become dissatisfied.

YOUR LIFE PHILOSOPHY

"Learn the rules, break the rules, make up new rules, break the new rules."

MARVIN BELL

When I left that coffee shop, I began to uncover what was going on with how I was experiencing life.

Simply put, I didn't feel the way I thought I was supposed to feel. The gap between my expectations and my reality had finally grown so wide and so deep that it was causing me to emotionally shut down.

Where did that gap come from?

Easy. The rules I told you about earlier.

Those rules I shared earlier were supposed to make me the person I was meant to be, do what I was meant to do, and feel happy. I was the mouse in a cage who was taught that if it hit the lever, cheese would come out.

I was the mouse.

The rules I thought I was supposed to live by were the levers.

A picture-perfect life and happiness were the cheese.

The problem was that "they" lied to me. I was hitting all the right levers, but there was no cheese.

Those rules were my life philosophy.

But there were other rules that were a part of my life philosophy I didn't know about. Unspoken rules.

When I look back, I can see these unspoken rules as the driving forces behind so many aspects of my life. Especially anything rooted in fear, anger, or loneliness. Only years later can I put these rules into words:

You are not loved.

You are not chosen.

You are alone.

If I was in a fight with my wife, it felt like a confirmation of my fear: I was unloved.

My desire to achieve was fueled by another fear: I wasn't chosen.

If I made a mistake, I feared people would leave me: I was alone.

These unspoken rules were written by the wounds, sufferings, and challenges I had experienced. They were buried so deep I didn't even know they were there.

Then there were the rules of the world. The world told me I needed pleasure. The world told me I needed power and prestige. The world told me I needed to be recognized. The world told me I needed to be successful. The world told me

I needed nice things and lots of money. The world told me I needed to look perfect.

These are the rules of the empty and afraid. The fundamentally unhappy. When you live by rules like this, like I did, nothing will ever be enough. It won't matter how much power or pleasure or money or how many experiences or positive vibes or accomplishments or possessions or people or anything else you amass. You will never be truly happy.

The problem is that you and I usually can't recognize these rules at first. If you had asked me before I started my journey to discover the Fundamental Theory of Happiness, I couldn't have put this stuff into words! This might be true for you now.

The Fundamental Theory of Happiness teaches you to discover and cast off these false philosophies and look for something better.

It's time to kill the false philosophies that hold you down.

Hey, are you with me?

What is your life philosophy?

Really consider the question. What are the ideas, thoughts, and values driving your life right now? What are the spoken rules? The unspoken rules? Write them down. Seriously. Write them down.

If you aren't sure, look back at key moments in your life and ask, "Why?"

You can ask "why" about anything.

Why did I buy a car I couldn't afford?

Why did I take that job?

Why did I date that person?

Why did I end a relationship with that person?

Why did I get angry?

Why do I always do this thing I don't want to do?

Why can't I stick to a budget?

Why can't I keep a job?

Why am I afraid to make decisions?

Why am I my own worst enemy?

As you look at your thoughts, decisions, actions, and habits, you will start to uncover patterns. Those patterns are your life philosophy.

Now comes the fun part. Circle all the rules that you believe are holding you back. The first step in overcoming anything is being able to name it—to call it out into the light. Circle it, own it, and stop letting it hide from you.

THE STRANGER IN THE MIRROR

"I do not understand my own actions. For I do not do what I want, but I do the very thing I hate."

ROMANS 7:15

When we are driven by false philosophies, we usually end up seeing two phenomena dominate our lives: The Stranger in the Mirror and The Man in the Mask.

Have you ever done something you didn't want to do or struggled to do something you wanted to do? Have you ever thought to yourself, *Why did I just do that? That's not me.*

This is The Stranger in the Mirror.

When I think of The Stranger in the Mirror, I think of Noah ...

I looked up from my desk as I made last-minute adjustments to that day's lesson plans, and there was Noah, standing in my doorway. But I didn't see the winning smile and carefree demeanor that made teachers love him and his classmates admire him. His hair fell over his face as he looked at his shoes, and he looked a few inches shorter than normal. I heard a small sniff, and I knew he was crying.

"Come on in, Noah." I might have been young, but I knew enough to not overreact, to not act panicked, and to ask what was wrong. I put my hand on his shoulder and led him to the seat nearest my desk. He fell into it, and I walked back to shut my office door.

I sat back down and waited. After a few minutes of silence, I said, "Noah, it's OK if you want to talk, and it's OK if you want to sit and not talk. I'm not going anywhere."

He had been waiting for the invitation. "Mr. Albano, I did something awful."

Then the details poured out.

Noah went to a party. Alcohol was involved. Noah's girlfriend wasn't there, but some students from another school were. There was a girl. First, they were smiling from across the room. Then they were dancing. Then they were kissing.

High school drama. It should have been nothing. But to Noah, it was much more, and I knew it.

I started as a campus counselor and moved into a teaching role, so I knew many of the students well. Noah had shared a lot with me. I tried to let my face be a mask. I thought about each of the muscles of my face and neck. I thought about my breathing. I didn't want to make things worse by reacting. Sometimes the best reassurance is to not be shocked, saddened, or sickened—simply to not react at all.

But inside I was remembering.

I remembered Noah telling me about the rotating men in his mother's life.

I remembered Noah telling me about when he finally stopped hoping his dad would come back.

I remembered Noah telling me how afraid he was that he would just repeat the mistakes of his parents.

I'll never forget his words as he finished his story: "I looked at myself in the mirror this morning, and I couldn't even recognize myself."

There have been many moments in my life when I have felt just like Noah. Times I've done things I never thought I would do. Times I thought, *If anyone knew the real me, they couldn't possibly love me.*

Why do we struggle to be the person we want to be or to do what we really want to do?

A Fundamental Truth:
Whenever we fail to do what we know is good
and true to who we are, that failure is driven
by the false philosophies of life.
Whenever we do what we know is not good and
not true to who we are, that failure is driven
by the false philosophies of life.

Maybe you know this feeling all too well. Maybe you know what it feels like to look at yourself in the mirror and not recognize the person you see. Maybe you've asked yourself, "How did this happen?"

If that's where you are now, I'm sorry. I've been there. It's terrible to be there. But there is a way out. It's not the end. Just hang on.

Hey, are you with me?

On a scale of 1–10, with 1 representing "almost never" and 10 representing "all the time," how often do you experience The Stranger in the Mirror?

1   2   3   4   5   6   7   8   9   10

O————————————————————————————O

THE MAN IN THE MASK

"Because true belonging only happens when we present our authentic, imperfect selves to the world, our sense of belonging can never be greater than our level of self-acceptance."

BRENÉ BROWN

Every single person you meet could point to at least one aspect of their life they wish was better.

It's health or finances. It's work or family. It's marriage or addiction. It's job loss or tragedy. Every single person you meet every single day is carrying a burden. We just don't talk about it.

Life gets hard, things go wrong, our plans don't work out, or we get hurt—but it seems like everyone else is just fine! So we put on a mask. A mask of happiness. Of fulfillment. Of perfection.

I've spent an hour counseling a husband in private about his broken marriage, and then seen him at church on Sunday with his wife, interacting with their friends like nothing was wrong. I've known people who were out of work and hid it from their spouse. I've counseled teens who were harming themselves, but around their friends they were the picture of fun and optimism.

Am I saying we should all walk around sharing our deepest fears and greatest burdens with everyone we meet?

No, not at all.

I am saying we should take off the mask. The more we wear the masks of happiness and fulfillment, the more we forget the truth. Eventually, we convince ourselves this is the best life has to offer.

But life has more to offer than a false image of happiness. You can have the real thing.

Hey, are you with me?

On a scale of 1–10, with 1 representing "almost never" and 10 representing "all the time," how often do you experience The Man in the Mask?

1   2   3   4   5   6   7   8   9   10

Neuroscience

SOCIAL MEDIA

Studies have shown that social media hurts face-to-face relationships, decreases participation in meaningful activities, leads to a sedentary lifestyle, creates internet addiction, and obliterates self-esteem.

When researchers from Yale University and UC San Diego began researching how Facebook use affects happiness, they expected to see that it had a negative effect on overall happiness, but they never predicted how bad it would be.

They studied participants over the course of two years, tracking information along the way. They set baselines for each individual regarding their typical daily Facebook use, overall physical health, overall mental health, life satisfaction, and happiness. Then they tracked each of those factors over a two-year period. Here's what they discovered:

The data showed that the digital relationships promoted by Facebook stunt happiness. And it wasn't just overall happiness that was harmed. While participants did show a significant decrease in life satisfaction and overall happiness, they showed an even larger decrease in mental and physical health.

Not only that, but the more participants used Facebook, the worse it got. They specifically found that the more you click links and like others' content, the more you will see a reduction in the four categories of overall well-being.

The study goes on to say that while they can definitively say that Facebook use seems to lead to diminished well-being, they don't know why.

But to be honest, I don't need to know. I've heard enough to conclude it's about time to get off social media.[1]

GETTING SEASICK

"We cannot solve our problems with the same thinking we used when we created them."

ALBERT EINSTEIN

I hate writing about this stuff. It disgusts me.

The lies we've been taught, the things we do that we wish we never did, the way we lie to ourselves and the world about what's really going on.

I hope you are saying to yourself—screaming to yourself— *there must be a better way!*

I hope you are completely dissatisfied with living another day like this.

Because you don't have to. There is a better way.

The truth is, we're all in the same boat, and we're all getting seasick. The people who are the best off are the ones who know it. They're the only ones who can do something about it.

It's OK if you are feeling a little uncomfortable. It's OK if you are feeling a little sick and tired of feeling sick and tired. In fact, it's good.

It means you are well on your way to living the first rule of the Fundamental Theory of Happiness for yourself: Become dissatisfied.

WHAT IS HAPPINESS?

*"I think everybody should get rich and famous
and do everything they ever dreamed of so they
can see that it's not the answer."*

JIM CARREY

My son Anthony has an insatiable appetite for life. You will not find an eight-year-old boy with more passion. He plays every baseball game like it's game seven of the World Series. It is impossible for him to come home at night without grass stains on his knees, sweat stains on his shirt, and at least one scrape.

Most nights he asks if I will come lie down with him. We cuddle on his bottom bunk, and he tells me stories and asks me questions.

One night he whispered, "Dad, why do we sleep?"

"We sleep so we can be healthy and have energy for tomorrow."

"Yeah, but why can't we just keep going? I don't like stopping all the fun stuff."

I sensed this was more than the musings of an eight-year-old boy who was trying to avoid having to fall asleep.

"Anthony, what makes you happy?"

"Baseball and video games and Legos and other stuff."

"How many baseball games will be enough?"

"What do you mean?"

"How many baseball games would you have to play to feel happy forever?"

"Like seven bajillion kazillion."

"So you are saying you'll never play enough baseball games to be really happy?"

Silence.

"I guess not."

"And how long would your mom and I have to let you play video games for you to feel happy forever?"

"Like, all day every day."

"So you are saying you'll never play enough video games to be really happy?"

Silence.

"I guess not."

"And how many Lego sets would you have to build to feel happy forever?"

"Like, all of the Lego sets ever."

"So you are saying you'll never have enough Lego sets to be really happy?"

Silence.

"I guess not."

Happiness is at the heart of every decision we make. We make the choices we make because we think they will lead us to happiness.

The problem with that?

A Fundamental Truth:
*If you are not happy before you have
or do something, you will not be happy
after you have it or do it.*

What you wear, what you drive, the house you own, the work you do, the accomplishments you achieve, the people you are friends with, the books you read, the experiences you have— none of it will *make* you happy.

Could any of that stuff make you *feel* happy? Sure. But no one struggles with *feeling* happy.

If you just needed to feel happy, this book could be a list of hundreds of one-line suggestions.

Eat a chocolate bar.

Take a nap.

Watch your favorite movie.

Call someone you love.

Get a massage.

And so on …

No, most people don't struggle with feeling happy. The problem comes down to *how long* they will feel happy. A candy bar will make you feel happy for a few minutes. A nap a few hours. For many people, the question becomes, How can I feel happy the longest?

And just like my son Anthony discovered that night lying in his bed, the truth is that none of the stuff we chase after to feel happy will last forever.

That's why the Fundamentally Happy are no longer concerned with feeling happy.

They're concerned with *being* happy. Because being happy and feeling happy are two very different things.

The fundamentally unhappy chase after happiness the way a dog chases a rabbit. Chasing after having and doing might make you feel happy, but the more you chase, the less happy you will be.

The Fundamentally Happy are different. They can have their possessions and achievements and riches and recognition stripped away and still be just as happy without them as they were with them.

Happiness isn't what you have or what you do. The Fundamental Theory of Happiness will not help you *feel* happy. It will help you *be* happy. And that makes all the difference.

Theory in Practice:
SELF-DENIAL

How often do you say "no" to yourself?

If you're like most people, the answer is "not very often."

Let's be honest about that. For most of us, if we want something, we can have it, and if it's not terrible for us, we have it.

If I want a soda with dinner, I have it.

If I want to adjust the thermostat by one degree, I do it.

If I want to veg out and watch TV after the kids go to bed, I do it.

We usually only say "no" to ourselves when we can't have something or shouldn't have something.

This Theory in Practice flies in the face of that. The goal is to find something you can have, that's not bad for you, and choose not to have it anyway.

Why does it matter? Because I want you to be free from the idea that feeling happy and being happy are the same thing. I want you to believe it, so I'm asking you to live it.

Your goal: Make one conscious decision every day for one week to deny yourself something you can have that's not bad for you.

Examples might include:

- Have a salad instead of a burger.
- Read instead of watch TV.
- Delay a purchase for a month.
- Give up coffee or alcohol for a week.
- Get up a half hour earlier than you need to.
- Take a cold shower (that one's the worst for me).
- Set the thermostat three degrees cooler (or warmer) than you'd like.

The list above gives some examples to start, but you will find others. Some days you'll have to plan it out. Other days the opportunity will present itself. But from now on, don't let a day go by without telling yourself "no."

A TIME TO KILL

"We are half-hearted creatures, fooling about with drink and sex and ambition when infinite joy is offered us, like an ignorant child who wants to go on making mud pies in a slum because he cannot imagine what is meant by the offer of a holiday at the sea. We are far too easily pleased."

C.S. LEWIS

Enough is enough. Now that you've identified them, it's time to kill the false philosophies. Cast out the stranger in the mirror. Take off the masks.

At the beginning of this chapter, I shared my first step toward becoming Fundamentally Happy. I became radically dissatisfied.

For months I battled feelings of emptiness. I thought it was me. I thought I was empty. I thought I wasn't doing life right. Until one night I realized it wasn't me. I realized that I had it backward the whole time.

My wife was lying under the covers, knees pulled up, Kindle tucked against her legs, with her back propped up against a ridiculous number of pillows. She has to read before falling asleep.

My head flopped onto my pillow next to her, and I let out a deep sigh, letting the backs of my hands come to rest over my eyes as exhaustion from the day rolled over me.

A hand caressed my forearm. "Great day, huh?"

I lifted my hand and peered through one squinted eye, confusion showing on my face. She didn't notice. She was still staring at her book.

The question was so casual it wasn't even a question. It was a statement in the form of a question.

"You think so?" I asked as casually as I could.

"Are you kidding? I can't remember the last time the boys had this much fun, and you weren't dragged into a hundred phone calls or emails throughout the weekend. I feel like we have so much more of you now."

We had spent the weekend together. Totally uninterrupted. We set up a tent in the backyard, played catch, went for walks, went to Mass together, got donuts after, played on our playground, read books … all of it. I didn't think of it like I was giving them any special gift. It was just the only time I didn't feel empty.

And then my wife said something that put all those memories out of my head.

"I can't remember the last time I saw you so happy."

I won't lie. At first, I wondered how she could be so impossibly disconnected from what was really going on inside me. But then I stopped. I listened. And I remembered that sometimes the people who are closest to us can see us better than we ever see ourselves.

I recalled the events of our weekend with a stark new realization. That empty feeling wasn't there. In fact, I was happy. I was happy the whole weekend.

So much of who I was and what I was living for was caught up in what I had, what I did, where I was going, and how I was going to get there that as soon as they seemed empty, I seemed empty.

I wasn't empty, everything I used to live for was. But I carried that empty feeling with me because I had let my possessions and ambitions become my identity.

And my wife, in her beautiful, simple wisdom, had shattered that.

That simple moment was a turning point in my life. A trigger moment in my search for happiness. Until that point, I had treated happiness like it was hiding. In that moment, when the masks were stripped away and the stranger in the mirror was gone and it was just me, I realized that all the stuff I was chasing to find happiness was actually the stuff holding me back from it.

I want you to learn that lesson too. I want you to have a true breakthrough in your own happiness.

I don't use the word breakthrough lightly. The world buries us in the things it says will make us happy. We live behind the veil and beneath the weight of this false philosopher. There is no gentle way out of it. There is no safe passage around it. We can only break through it.

The world wants you to chase after comfort and mediocrity, and it tells you those things will make you happy. But those are lies. They'll just hold you back from it.

It's time to become radically dissatisfied with comfort and mediocrity.

A Fundamental Truth:
At the end of their life, most people do not find that they wanted too much. Most find that they settled for far too little.

You were made for more than comfort and mediocrity. Don't settle for it. It's easy and it gets in the way of your happiness.

True happiness, now that's something worth wanting.

Hey, are you with me?

Everyone sacrifices lasting happiness for temporary comfort sometimes. Most of us have those things we turn to. Maybe it's television, food, social media, or alcohol. Maybe it's a possession. Maybe it's something else. List five things you turn to when you give in to comfort and mediocrity. Naming them will help you be conscious of how you trade happiness for comfort.

1. _____

2. _____

3. _____

4. _____

5. _____

Neuroscience

THE LITTLE THINGS

Researchers from New York University's Stern School of Business conducted a study to test a simple observation of human nature.

If you knew you had to endure a painful experience for thirty minutes, and you were offered to take a short break during the time, would you accept? Absolutely. Everyone would.

If you knew you were going to enjoy a pleasurable experience for thirty minutes, and you were offered to take a short break during the time, would you accept? Absolutely not. Nobody would.

The basic assumption is that the break will make the painful experience less painful and the pleasurable experience less pleasurable. Pretty straightforward. The researchers wanted to know if this assumption was true.

According to the research, at play in this study is the fact that our experiences either increase in intensity (sensitization) or decrease in intensity (adaptation). When we choose to take a break from the painful experience, it is because we believe the break will decrease the intensity. We deny the break from the pleasurable experience because we fear the break will decrease the intensity. But the research shows we have this all wrong.

Adaptation decreases the intensity of an experience, making the painful less painful and the pleasurable less pleasurable. Bottom line: We get used to the pain or the pleasure, so we feel it less. But the break prevents us from adapting. It's totally counterintuitive, but the break actually makes the pain worse because it prevents us from getting used to it, and it makes the pleasure increase for the same reason!

Turns out, the enemy of happiness is adaptation. The enemy of happiness is getting used to it!

Participants reported higher levels of happiness across the board when experiencing frequent little boosts to their happiness, as compared to less frequent larger boosts.

Why do new cars, a new house, long vacations, a new promotion, and all the other big boosts to happiness so easily fade and fail to increase our overall happiness? Because we get used to them! We adapt!

If you want to be happier, don't look for the rare and big things (the cars, the trips, the new house) … their allure will fade. It turns out the little things will beat them out every time.

Step II:
A Deeper Perception

IMAGINE

*"Those who are able to see beyond the shadows
and lies of their culture will never be understood,
let alone believed, by the masses."*

PLATO

Imagine:

People can't figure you out. You do the same work, live in the same town, shop at the same stores, and have the same ups and downs—but everything seems to work differently for you.

For one, not much bothers you. Whether life goes wrong or right, you're the same person. In difficult times, when someone else might implode, you're calm and collected. It's like you have an inner strength keeping you up.

People feel like you know something they don't. You're generous, but somehow no matter how much you give, you end up with more. You know exactly what you want and aren't swayed by jealousy or cheap thrills. Your friends, family, coworkers, and neighbors feel like the world conspires to make things work in your favor.

You see the world differently. No one understands exactly what it is you've got … but they know they want it.

THE FIVE LEVELS OF PERCEPTION

*"Everything can be taken from a man but one thing;
the last of the human freedoms—to choose one's attitude in
any given set of circumstances, to choose one's own way."*
VIKTOR FRANKL

What would you do?

You're driving home from work, minding your own business, when a guy in a blue sedan comes flying across two lanes of traffic and cuts you off to make the next exit. If you're like most people, you're probably outraged at the dangerous maneuver and can't help thinking, *What a jerk!* (Or let's be honest, you probably think something much worse.)

It's been nearly three weeks since the family a few houses down from yours last mowed their lawn. At first you thought they were away on vacation because you weren't seeing them around the house or their cars in the driveway. Now the place looks totally disheveled. The two-foot tall grass and weeds look terrible, and you can't help but wonder what kind of people let their home fall into such disarray.

These reactions are understandable, but how would this change things?

That guy who cut you off was driving his wife to the hospital because she was in labor prematurely.

The husband from the family down the street—the husband you typically wave to as he mows his lawn on the weekend—has been in the hospital the last three weeks. He's been diagnosed with a rare form of cancer, and his family has spent almost every waking moment at the hospital with him since his diagnosis.

Would those details change your reaction?

Circumstances matter. What we know or don't know makes a difference. In both those scenarios, you would react differently because of the circumstances. You'd gladly get out of the way of the car. You'd walk down the street and mow the lawn to help in some small way.

Now imagine if you could have that kind of patient, knowing, understanding reaction to every person and situation around you, without needing to know the extenuating circumstances.

The Fundamentally Happy have this power. Nothing seems to bother them, and it always seems like they know something we don't know.

I've taken the Fundamentally Happy way of seeing the world and converted it into actionable steps you can start practicing. But first, let's see which of the five levels of perception and reaction you're living at now.

First off, life is busy. You're probably moving from the moment you wake up until the moment you go to bed. From an important work meeting, to your daughter's dance recital, to your son's hockey game, to the church's finance council meeting. And don't forget that important deadline on your big project, getting the yard mowed, coaching soccer, and getting the oil changed on the car. That all needs to get done before lunch.

And then there are the constant voicemails, text messages, and emails. This is real life, and it doesn't even include other important aspects like planning for the future, maintaining a healthy relationship with your spouse, taking care of yourself physically and spiritually, or finding time to re-energize and focus.

Herein lies the problem: The real life we're living feels like it's holding us back from really living life. We're like the entrepreneur who is so wrapped up in running the business that he can't step back for a moment without everything falling to pieces.

How do the Fundamentally Happy turn this all around? It all comes down to what you respond to. What you respond to determines at what level you live your life.

Life is lived at essentially five different levels: effect, cause, circumstances, intentions, and purpose.

Consider this scenario:

I'm walking through the door much later than I was supposed to be. I know my wife wants me home by a certain time, but today my boss made me stay late to work because of a missed deadline, and then I got caught in bad traffic on the way home. I'm expecting she's going to be angry before I even walk in the door.

EFFECT

At this level we only see and respond to effects. The fundamentally unhappy are usually stuck at this level. When we're here, we are swallowed up in emotions, crisis, drama, and fear. We move from fire to fire feeling like life is a runaway train and the bridge is out. This is surface-level living. We can't see past the physical.

Example: My wife's angry. If I react at this level, I'm going to respond to her anger with matching anger.

CAUSE

Scraping just below the effect, now we can also see the causes. At this level, we see the action, behavior, or thought that causes the effect, but we're still consumed by the physical: what we see and experience. It's important to note that at these first two levels, our reactions are entirely inward focused. There is a lack of empathy.

Example: My wife is angry because I came home late from work.

CIRCUMSTANCE

Now we fall back on the circumstances surrounding the cause and effect. People on this level are starting to enter into an empathic mindset, but they still blame any wrongdoing on their circumstances rather than take any personal responsibility. It's still about me, not the other person. You're deeper than cause and effect, but not much.

Example: I'm home late because my boss made this last-minute adjustment to a project I had to get done by the end of the day, and then there was an accident on the highway that blocked up traffic.

INTENTION

The level of intention takes us to a deeper level of empathy and understanding. We usually judge ourselves and our actions on this level. I didn't mean to be late; I wasn't trying to hurt you! When we make a mistake, we justify our actions based on our intentions. When others make a mistake, we tend to judge only the cause and effect. This is the first level that has any real care for the other person.

Example: I'm sorry, I didn't mean to be home late! I wanted to be home on time.

PURPOSE

This is the deepest level at which we can live. The person who responds to purpose sees things differently. Here live the motivations, drivers, and desires at the heart of everything. Full empathy happens on this level. You aren't focused on what you are experiencing, you're focused on the other person.

Example: Part of my purpose as a husband is to be a trustworthy and accountable companion who makes my wife feel secure and safe. When I show up late, I break trust, and I have to figure out a way—despite circumstances that are outside of my control—to make sure my wife knows her safety and security are priorities to me.

Putting our example in another sense:

The person living at the level of effect says, "You're angry at me?!"

The person living at the level of cause says, "You think I wanted to be home late from work?" (Is this starting to sound like the script to some of the most common fights between married couples?)

The person living at the level of circumstance says, "I'm sorry there was a traffic jam and my boss made me stay late."

The person living at the level of intention says, "I'm sorry, I didn't mean to be home late."

The person living at the level of purpose says, "I'm sorry I wasn't the dependable husband you need me to be. In the future, I can try to call ahead of time to make you more aware of what's going on, and to see if there is anything I can do to make your night easier considering I'll be home late. Is there anything I can do now? I'd be happy to do it."

Is this example a bit simplified? Absolutely. But it illustrates the point. Apologizing for not being the husband you should be might be a little extreme for something as simple as being home a little late, but you never know.

Bottom line: The Fundamentally Happy live at the level of purpose. This is the second rule of the Fundamental Theory of Happiness.

Why does it seem like they know something we don't know?

Why does it seem like the world conspires in their favor?

The answer is perception.

The Fundamentally Happy aren't responding to the effects in their lives. They are looking beyond the surface and living life according to purpose.

The weather, the searing emotions from their boss, the downturn in the economy, the new tech everyone has to have, the traffic jam on their commute, the annoying coworker, their favorite team having a miserable season ... these effects don't shake them.

Living at the level of purpose allows the Fundamentally Happy to be proactive instead of reactive.

Imagine you are having a problem with a coworker.

If you are reactive, you might become emotional, angry, or fearful. You might start playing the blame game or trying to fix the problem, only to see the coworker is still being difficult. We've all encountered people who always find something to be upset about. All of these responses are reactive: reacting to the causes, effects, circumstances, and intentions. Now compare this to the Fundamentally Happy.

The Fundamentally Happy will immediately begin to search for the purpose of the person and the situation. What are we trying to accomplish here? What's the purpose of this person, this project? What's at the heart of this conflict? The Fundamentally Happy will work from the purpose of one aspect to the next—from the person to the conflict—to understand at the deepest level.

When you know your purpose, you know what you're responsible for and who you're responsible to. You might be able to stop an argument by addressing effect, cause, circumstances, or intention, but until you address the deepest level, you can't have lasting change.

Living at the level of purpose transforms everything.

Problems with your kids?

Ask yourself what is your child's purpose, what is the purpose of children, and what is the purpose of parenthood? What is your purpose as a parent?

Problems with a relationship?

Ask yourself what is your partner's purpose? What is your purpose in the relationship? What is the purpose of being in a relationship?

Problems with your health?

Ask yourself what is the purpose of your body? Of yourself?

Problems with your money?

Ask yourself what is the purpose of money?

You might be thinking you have no idea what your purpose is, or what your spouse's purpose is, or what your children's purpose is. That's great.

You're starting to think like the Fundamentally Happy.

Theory in Practice:
ASSUME THE BEST

There's an old-fashioned lesson on Christian duty that has fallen out of practice today.

Assume the best about other people.

We have a tendency to suspect and jump to conclusions. Gossip, rumor mongering, paranoia, and snap judgements are our new normal.

The guy cuts you off on the highway because he's a jerk, right? We don't think we need to know anything else.

But we rarely know the circumstances and intentions of those around us, so assume the best—if not for their benefit, then for your own. You could be annoyed for your whole day if someone cuts you off in traffic. It can make you feel like people are jerks and the world is nasty. But if you assume the best, say a quick prayer for the person, and wish them safety on their way, it changes the whole interaction. I promise, you will feel happier.

For one week, try to assume the best about those around you. If you succeed, it's likely to be one of the best weeks you've had in a while.

THE POVERTY OF OUR TIMES

> *"In order to understand the world, one has to turn away from it on occasion."*
> ALBERT CAMUS

Every firstborn son in my family is named either Dominick Louis or Anthony Louis. My firstborn son is Anthony Louis. I'm Dominick Louis. My father is Anthony Louis. My grandfather is Dominick Louis, and so on. It's a proud family tradition.

My grandfather, Dominick Louis Albano, passed on January 20, 2015. He was a World War II veteran, married my grandmother on their fourth date, worked hard his entire life as a construction worker and foreman, built his house with his own bare hands, raised five children in that house, and loved his wife for seventy-one years. He drove a Cadillac and loved Duke basketball, the Yankees, and bowling. He was a titan of a man; the kind of patriarch that—though you knew he loved you—you were a little bit afraid of.

Before Grandpop died, my uncle (also Dominick Louis Albano) had interviewed him and Grandmom and filmed them sharing stories about their life. After Grandpop's funeral, I sat down with my family to hear their stories.

My grandfather only had one shirt and pants in high school. He washed them every other night to stay presentable. He got his start as an Army Air Corps radio control man and met Grandmom while training in Arizona before being deployed in World War II. He married her on their fourth date.

But more than all this, one simple question caught my attention. My uncle asked him what he did for fun while he was in high school.

My grandfather's answer? Nothing.

Fun? He almost seemed incredulous at the idea.

> "We didn't have television or computers like you all have today. At night we just sat around on the front porch until it was time to go to sleep!"

Have you ever noticed how different real stillness feels?

That feeling as you sit on your porch at dawn on a summer day? Or when you sit alone in an empty church? Or when you go for a walk along a long stretch of deserted beach?

This kind of silence and solitude are at an all-time low in our society, and they are absolutely essential to living at the level of purpose. Why? Without silence or solitude, we can't think. It's as simple as that.

Have you ever been dealing with a difficult problem you couldn't get your head around and then, when you weren't even thinking about it, the solution falls into place? Or have you ever looked so deep into a situation you could see it from someone else's perspective? Or reached a new level of understanding watching a situation from outside yourself? Or maybe your mind wandered and suddenly you had an insight or clarification?

A Fundamental Truth:
Silence and solitude are essential
for finding your purpose.

This is why Grandpop's answer jumped at me. Although he grew up through the Great Depression, there was one great poverty I grew up with that he didn't. A poverty of silence and solitude.

I've grown up in the age of computers, cell phones, twenty-four-hour television, shower radios, iPods, earbuds, car radios, and so many other sources of noise and distraction. Silence and solitude aren't just rare in our society, they are difficult to find even if you want them.

This poverty has made the ability to think deeply a lost art.

This is the skill I try to implore every young person I meet to develop.

If you can think deeply, it's like you can see the future. You'll have wisdom beyond your years, and your thoughts and words will carry a weight that others won't. Your opinions will be respected more than others, people will be drawn to you, and you will have more clarity and focus than those around you. This ability will benefit every part of your life, from your relationships to your work, from your health and well-being to your intellectual prowess and spiritual life.

The best part about silence, solitude, and the subtle art of thinking deeply is that no one needs to teach you how. You don't need to purchase any memberships. You don't need a master's degree. Just drive to your local church and sit alone in silence. It might be a little uncomfortable at first, but in time you won't just be comfortable in the silence and solitude, you will yearn for it.

I was probing a Fundamentally Happy friend of mine about the role of silence and solitude in his life. He confirmed that it is essential to how he lives his life, that he builds intentional time for silence and solitude into his daily routine—sometimes even getting up at four in the morning to seek it out.

Where did he learn the value of silence and solitude? From hunting with his father. He says the life he lives, the success he has experienced, and the depth at which he lives all go back to his time hunting.

While his friends were at home surrounded by video games and televisions and noise, he was up in a tree stand in the middle of a farmer's field, alone, with nothing but silence and solitude. It was there he learned to think deeply. He would spend hours thinking about one simple idea or exploring just one question. He had silence and solitude before he even knew how important it was, and it has made all the difference in his life.

Hey, are you with me?

Where do you find silence and solitude in your life?

_____

_____

_____

When was the last time you thought deeply about something?

_____

_____

_____

How you answer these questions will reveal at what level you're currently living, which will reveal how happy you are.

Theory in Practice:
GO HUNTING (METAPHORICALLY)

The goal is silence and solitude. The rules are simple:

1. **Be alone.** No kids, no spouse, no friend, no roommate. Alone.

2. **Eliminate the distractions.** No phone, television, music, computers, smart watches, or anything else tempting. Go in the basement, under the stairs, in the garage, in the bathroom, anywhere you have to go to escape distractions.

3. **Don't do anything.** In the eyes of the world, this will be a complete waste of time.

4. **Stay for ten minutes.** Do it every day for a week—at least.

At first it will be awkward and uncomfortable. You might feel silly. It might feel like a waste of time. Give it a few days. Soon enough, you won't just be comfortable, you will yearn for the silence.

You will be amazed by what a little bit of solitude can do in your life.

Neuroscience

TIME

Researchers from Stanford University and the University of Pennsylvania were tired of seeing inconclusive research reports trying to figure out the relationship between happiness and money. Over and over again, reports showed that there was no statistical correlation between making more money and being happier, but researchers just kept going back to the topic. So the researchers from Stanford and the University of Pennsylvania decided to look someplace else.

Time.

While no statistical evidence has been found to link how we spend our money to our happiness, these researchers found five principles of spending time that had a statistical correlation to increased happiness.

Based on their findings, they suggest five time-spending happiness principles.

1. **Spend time with the right people.**

   Their research showed that happiness levels increase with spending time with the right people: family and close friends. They also noted that because most people spend a significant amount of time at work, individuals who reported having a "best friend" at work and individuals who liked their boss had higher levels of reported happiness than those who didn't.

2. **Spend time on the right activities.**

   Will what I am doing right now become more valuable
   over time? This question alone increased the chances
   that participants would experience more happiness.
   The question reoriented participants' activities to
   something that gave energy and enthusiasm, and it
   helped participants get through important obligations
   (like paying bills and cleaning) faster.

3. **Enjoy activities without actually doing them.**

   Neuroscience research has revealed that—in certain
   activities—merely thinking about an experience creates
   the same happy feelings as the experience itself. The
   researchers suggest that merely thinking about a happy
   activity like drinking a favorite local beer or driving a
   favorite sports car can increase our happiness just as
   much as actually doing it. Furthermore, the research
   showed that the increase in happiness experienced
   from planning and anticipating activities like a
   vacation or eating out at a restaurant had statistically
   higher positive effects on happiness than the actual
   experience of the vacation or eating at the restaurant.

4. **Expand your time.**

   Time is a limited resource. You can't make any more than twenty-four hours in a day. But focusing on the future made participants feel like they had less time than participants who were told to focus on the present. Participants who focused on the present moment actually felt like time slowed down. Participants who were told to take long slow breaths for five minutes reported feeling like their day was longer and they had more time to get things done than participants who were told to take quick short breaths for five minutes.

5. **Be aware that happiness changes over time.**

   The experiences and feelings people associate with happiness change over time. Younger participants reported associating happiness more with excitement, whereas older participants reported associating happiness more with peace. The important thing here: The changes in how we perceive happiness follow patterns. The researchers concluded that if you learn to predict how your perception of happiness will change, then you can spend your time more wisely to reap the greatest benefit.[2]

BROKEN CLOCKS

*"Somehow we human beings are never happier than when
we are expressing the deepest gifts that are truly us."*

OS GUINNESS

It had been 7:38 PM for a very long time.

I was sitting on my ugly brown recliner staring at a dead clock—one of those beauties with the octagonal face encased in wood and a brass pendulum swinging behind the glass. It had belonged to my wife's grandmother.

I was sitting in silence and solitude and—as usually happens in silence and solitude—my mind wandered to life's biggest questions:

Who am I?

What am I supposed to do with my life?

My wife was at work, and we didn't have kids yet. Life was simple and good, but a lot had happened in the past year.

In less than one year, we graduated college, got married, started careers, and bought a house. Life was happening fast.

As I sat and considered all these changes and life's big questions, my mind opened to whatever heaven had to say. That was when the clock spoke to me. Not in words, but in a moment of clarity that struck with such ferocity that my heartbeat quickened and my mind raced.

It was so simple. The clock was broken, but it was still a clock. It might have stopped performing its function, but that didn't mean it stopped being a clock. My eyes widened with dawning comprehension.

We don't know it's a clock because of what it's doing; we know it's a clock because of what it is supposed to do. Because of its purpose. A broken clock is still a clock.

Imagine someone didn't know what a clock was. They point at the wall and ask, "What is that?"

Would you say, "Well, that's a collection of gears, springs, and bolts that are turned by an oscillating pendulum encased in wood which turns a time-dial over a display with measured intervals that are distinguished by the numbers one through twelve"?

Um, I don't think so. That's its functions and features.

You'd probably say, "Oh, that's a clock. It tells the time." And then you might say, "Duh."

You would define the clock by its purpose.

Think about how different a clock can be in look, feel, size, wearability, and so on. Function and features can change, but they are all clocks. You'd still define the clock by its purpose.

What do we say when someone asks, "Who are you?"

We might talk about our past, our family, where we live, where we work (that's a favorite for most people). We might give our name, our preferences, our hobbies, our personality type, our favorite sports team, or something else along those lines. But that's the equivalent of telling someone all of our functions and features.

A Fundamental Truth:
We define everything in the world by its purpose.
Except ourselves.

Sitting in my ugly recliner that night at 7:38 PM (it wasn't actually 7:38 PM), I stumbled upon a crucial flaw in how I saw myself and every other person I knew. I saw myself, and everyone else, for my parts and not for my purpose.

But that was going to change.

Hey, are you with me?

Circle the words you would use if someone asked you, "Who are you?"

CAREER   WHERE YOU LIVE   HUSBAND   WIFE

FATHER   MOTHER   DEMOCRAT   REPUBLICAN

FAVORITE TEAM   COACH   ATHLETE

What else? Do you drive a motorcycle? Play golf? Paint? Take a few minutes and list any other words you usually use to describe yourself to others.

THE OBSESSION OF THE FUNDAMENTALLY HAPPY

"True happiness ... is not attained through self-gratification, but through fidelity to a worthy purpose."

HELEN KELLER

When we think about purpose, we usually wonder "Why am I here?" or "What am I supposed to do?"

But these questions will get you about as far as a racecar gets during a race: 500 miles in circles.

Looking at the broken clock, contemplating purpose on the deepest level, I discovered a better question: What was I made for?

This is the obsession of the Fundamentally Happy. It is the key to unlocking the question of purpose.

If you allow what you have or do to define your purpose, you are well on the path to being fundamentally unhappy. What you can or cannot do tells you nothing about who you really are. The sooner you get really clear on that, the sooner you can discover your true purpose.

Albert Einstein is attributed as saying, "Don't judge a fish by its ability to climb a tree." It's true. But Albert is only partially right. You also can't judge a fish by its ability to swim. Because purpose goes deeper than what you have or what you do.

Purpose can only be found in what you were made for.

If you are going to discover your purpose, you have to discover what you were made for.

Step III:
Face Your Enemies

THE SNEAK ATTACK

"If you know the enemy and know yourself, you need not fear the result of a hundred battles. If you know yourself but not the enemy, for every victory gained you will also suffer a defeat. If you know neither the enemy nor yourself, you will succumb in every battle."

SUN TZU

When I was a kid, I used to play capture the flag. Generally speaking, there were two offensive theories when it came to capture the flag.

The first was the open attack. This meant the fastest kid on the team would simply try to beat everyone with his speed. His attack was predictable and easily thwarted.

The other approach was the sneak attack. I had one friend who would crawl on his belly through the tall grass, creeping closer and closer to the flag until he would jump up, grab the flag, and be back on our side before anyone even knew what had happened.

Whether it's in capture the flag or in life, the most dangerous enemies are the ones we don't know exist.

Have you ever wondered, *Why can't I just be happy?*

This one thing has persisted through every stage of my journey to fundamental happiness. An inescapable truth that you have experienced too, even if you haven't recognized it.

Our lives are filled with enemies to our happiness.

Ever feel like life is working against you? Like things won't get better? Ever choose something you know will make you unhappy, or fail to choose something you know will make you happy? Ever feel afraid? Ever feel like it's the best you can do to just survive?

I debated when to bring these enemies up. I didn't want to speak about them too early, lest they discourage you on the journey. I didn't want to speak about them too late, lest they devour your energy and zeal to implement the Fundamental Theory of Happiness for yourself.

Now is the time.

I hope you are encouraged by some of the principles and have begun implementing them. I'm also willing to bet you've had enough time to experience some resistance—pushback to your quest for something better.

And that's great because if you've experienced the enemy, you will take this chapter seriously. It also means you know your enemy exists.

The battle is where the glory is won, and there are battles to fight when it comes to the Fundamental Theory of Happiness.

Get ready to face your enemies.

CORRUPTION

"For the desires of the flesh are against the Spirit,
and the desires of the Spirit are against the flesh;
for these are opposed to each other, to prevent you
from doing what you would."

GALATIANS 5:17

The education and formation of children is the foundation of any healthy society. If you want to know where a society is going, look to its efforts to raise up men and women of character, virtue, compassion, intelligence, and fortitude.

I'm a father, a godfather, an uncle, a baseball coach, and a neighbor. I interact with kids on a daily basis, and I care deeply about helping children and teenagers figure out life.

The first enemy deals directly with the most important thing you can teach a young person: the art of decision making.

They might not like it, but young people need help making decisions. If you put my children in a room with a thousand dollars' worth of toys and one exposed outlet, they will head straight for the outlet. Healthy play and disciplined work have a tough time competing against Netflix. As we get older, other decisions emerge. Who will we spend time with, what will we invest our time in, and what kind of future will we build for ourselves?

Over time we need to take more and more responsibility for our choices. If we have been formed in the art of making great decisions, we have a gift that will last a lifetime.

But even if we've been given all that, we will make choices that don't lead to our happiness. How do I know? Because I've been there. I've seen others make poor decisions. I've made those poor decisions myself.

I will never cease to be amazed and infuriated by my desire to choose things I know will make me unhappy and my resistance to choosing things I know will make me happy. The truth is, sometimes I'm my own worst enemy.

And this brings us to the name of our first enemy: our corrupt desires.

Why is it so easy to procrastinate yet it takes so much discipline to focus on work?

Why is it so easy to be lazy and so hard to keep a routine of exercise?

Why is it I can binge-watch entire seasons of a show but have to work hard to read a book?

In life, the easiest and most pleasurable thing is always more attractive in the short term.

A Fundamental Truth:
The easiest and most attractive things in the
short term will never lead to happiness.

If I could change anything about this world, that would be it. I would make the easiest and most attractive thing the choice that would lead us to happiness. But as it is, the easiest and most attractive thing is always the path of the fundamentally unhappy.

Now, it should be noted that, for the most part, the object of our desire itself is not bad or wrong, but it represents an interior motivation that will not lead to happiness.

For example, eating junk food is always easier and more attractive in the short term than eating healthy food, but that doesn't make junk food evil. If I'm having a family movie night, you better bet that each of us is chowing down on our favorite movie treat.

On the flip side, some people do "good" deeds or make "healthy" choices just for the pleasure of holding it over friends and family. For the most part, that attractive "thing" we desire is not good or evil, it's the motivation behind it that leads to unhappiness. Our corrupt desire is the true enemy.

To defeat this enemy, we have to figure out how to make the best decisions in spite of our corrupted desires.

The Fundamentally Happy have figured out how to master this enemy. Their weapon? Habits.

It's a simple and brilliant strategy. The Fundamentally Happy remove themselves from the decision-making process by building such strong habits that their actions become automatic.

They have physical habits. The Fundamentally Happy person has built up such a strong habit of running, for example, that it has become automatic. They no longer have to battle to get motivated, they just do it.

They have emotional habits. They have practiced honesty, kindness, humility, patience, self-control, and other virtues to the point that these are their default behaviors.

They have intellectual habits. The Fundamentally Happy build time into their day for reading, learning, creativity, and stimulation. Growth and stimulation are not left to chance.

They have spiritual habits. They have a set time, place, and routine for prayer. They go to Mass and serve in their community. These activities are consistent and automatic because they are habits.

In his book *The Power of Habit*, author Charles Duhigg says there is a very specific neurological process that habits are built on:

This process within our brains is a three-step loop. First, there is a cue, a trigger that tells your brain to go into automatic mode and which habit to use. Then there is the routine, which can be physical or mental or emotional. Finally, there is a reward, which helps your brain figure out if this particular loop is worth remembering for the future. Over time, this loop—cue, routine, reward; cue, routine, reward—becomes more and more automatic. The cue and reward become intertwined until a powerful sense of anticipation and craving emerges.[3]

How do you harness the power of this neurological process? You create new habits and rewrite old ones.

If you want to create a new habit, craft a cue, a routine, and a reward for that behavior.

Let's use creating a running habit as an example.

1. **Create a cue.** Putting socks and running shoes next to your bed.

2. **Create a reward.** The dopamine release experienced from exercise is its own reward, but throwing in a little something extra never hurts—a delicious post-run smoothie, let's say.

3. **Create routine.** You wake up, you see the shoes, you anticipate the reward. Repeat until the routine happens automatically.

If you want to rewrite an old bad habit, Duhigg tells us you must identify the cue and the reward, and work to rewrite the routine. Not always easy to do, but by growing in awareness, you can harness the power of habits to live a better life.

Take some time and bring your corrupt desire out into the light. What thoughts and behaviors attract you even though you know they are bad for you? What thoughts and behaviors do you struggle to choose even though you know they are good for you?

Once you identify the thoughts and behaviors you want to eliminate and the thoughts and behaviors you want to build up, figure out the "cue, routine, reward" habit loop for each, and write up a plan to tackle them.

But don't try to do everything at once. Rewriting old habits and creating new ones is simple, but simple doesn't mean easy. It takes time and repetition. The Fundamentally Happy are in it for the long haul. Take your time. Identify one habit at a time and work on that one until the new habit or routine is firmly established.

What's the secret to mastering the moment of decision and taking down the first enemy to your happiness? Take yourself and your corrupted desires out of the equation.

Neuroscience

SOCIAL MEDIA AND ADDICTION

Over two billion people use some form of social media. Increasingly, research is looking at the neuronal circuits activated while engaging in social media, as well as the psychological effects of using social media.

Much of the current research looks at the "Like" feature on most social media platforms, which provides people with instant, quantitative feedback. Receiving positive feedback on social media, or receiving a "Like," has been shown to activate the nucleus accumbens (NAc) and the ventral tegmental area (VTA), areas of the brain that play a central role in the reward circuit.[4] The NAc and VTA are not only activated when someone "Likes" our post, but also when we "Like" someone else's post.[5]

The reward circuit is driven by the neurotransmitter dopamine. Dopamine is released when we eat something delicious, exercise, and yes, when someone "Likes" our photo or post. It is this release of dopamine that provides instant gratification, rewards our social media behaviors, and motivates us to continue doing them.

But dopamine and the reward circuit also play a major role in addiction. The dopamine that is released activates the same neuronal pathways not only when someone "Likes" your photo, but also when someone does drugs or gambles. So if you have ever wondered why you are constantly checking your phone to see how many people "Liked" your photo, dopamine release and the brain's reward circuit are partially to blame.

Theory in Practice:
MAKE A LIST

Know Your Weaknesses

If you were going to storm a castle, you'd look for the weak point in the walls. If you were going to defend a castle, you'd put your best men on the weakest point. Makes sense, right?

Here's the thing: We have to get a handle on our weaknesses.

Make a list: Sit down for a half hour and make a list of your weak spots. Your list will be very personal. Some things that tempt me won't tempt you at all, and vice versa. Where are the enemies of your happiness likely to get you? Put another way, what are the things you sometimes do even though you know they won't make you happy?

Maybe it's gossip.

Maybe it's feelings of self-doubt or loathing.

Maybe it's laziness.

Maybe it's sexual temptations.

Maybe it's a bad temper.

We all have stuff like this, and we all wish we didn't. As much as we might be tempted to deny or hide it away, trust me, it's better to bring it into the light. Either you own this kind of stuff, or it owns you.

Get to know the weak spots in your defenses so you can bolster your guard.

OPPOSITION

*"Your friends will determine the quality
and direction of your life."*
ANDY STANLEY

Have you ever noticed that some people just make life easier? They get things done, they figure out problems, they reduce stress, and they maintain a positive and productive attitude. They are encouraging and driven. They are full of life, and you feel energized when you are around them.

On the other hand, have you ever noticed how some people just make life difficult? They only see problems, they complicate things, they create obstacles and roadblocks, and their attitude can sometimes be mean, angry, and difficult.

This second group isn't fun to be around, plain and simple. We want to be like that first group: a powerful influence for good for the people around us.

The influences we surround ourselves with are important. Why? Because of our next enemy: opposition. Specifically, opposition from the world and other people.

While most of us would like to believe the world and the people in it are good and have good intentions, experience doesn't align with that belief. There are forces in this life, seen and unseen, that do not have our best interest at heart.

These forces could be as simple as a discouraging coworker, a gossiping PTO member at our kids' school, or an unkind neighbor. Are these people evil? Of course not. Do they mean you harm? Probably not. Should you love them and try to be a source of good in their lives? Absolutely. But they can become a source of negative influence in your life if you aren't careful. The more you interact with these people, the less energy you have. You might begin to feel frustrated and tired. Your outlook might turn sour.

There are also many faceless forces that work against us. Consumerism and materialism are great examples. The culture cries for us to buy more, newer, bigger. Spend, spend, spend. These false values have put people into debt, driven them into a deep discontentment with life, and made the least important things into the most important things.

While some people might be put off by talk of dark or evil forces in the world, we only need to turn on the nightly news to see the horrific evidence of these unseen forces.

Our friends, family, coworkers, neighbors, the books we read, the shows we watch, the music we listen to, the things we buy, and so many other parts of life all play a part.

How do the Fundamentally Happy defeat this opposition? They recognize its power and are intentional about harnessing positive influences in their lives.

Surrounding yourself with the right kind of influences isn't always easy. We can't escape some people or parts of our culture. But there are two tactics employed by the Fundamentally Happy to help: awareness and filtering.

Awareness is the ability to recognize and evaluate the forces around you and how vulnerable you are to different types of influences. You might be more influenced by materialism than by negative people in your life. Or maybe you have a weakness for gossip. Maybe it's bad foods or television or music. When you recognize the forces you are most vulnerable to, you can raise your defenses in that area.

Filtering is the ability to open the floodgates to the best influences in your life and slam the door on bad influences.

This skill must be nurtured over time. Because of your first enemy (corrupt desire), it is likely that you probably desire some of the negative influences in your life. Filtering is about surrounding yourself with the influences that propel you toward your goals, aspirations, dreams, desired habits, and life skills.

So where do you start? Look for mentors. Build solid relationships and limit bad ones. Watch what you buy. Only read, watch, and listen to the things that build you up.

Bottom line: If you want to be Fundamentally Happy, go spend time around the Fundamentally Happy. Life moves in the direction of your influences.

Hey, are you with me?

Take a look at the following list.

Put an "X" through the thing that is easier.

Circle the thing that is good for you.

GOING FOR A RUN	SITTING ON THE COUCH
WATCHING NETFLIX	READING A BOOK
PRAYING	BEING BUSY
GOSSIPING	HOLDING YOUR TONGUE
WORKING HARD	BEING LAZY
HITTING SNOOZE	GETTING UP WHEN THE ALARM GOES OFF

Next, write the name of someone who supports you in doing what is good for you:

_____

Neuroscience

RELATIONSHIPS

In 1938, researchers at Harvard University began tracking the health and well-being of 268 university sophomores. The group included a young John F. Kennedy and future Washington Post editor Ben Bradlee. The researchers planned to study the longtime health and well-being of these men and—here's the crazy part—the study is still going on today.

Nineteen of the original recruits are still alive, but scientists at the university branched out over the years to include the wives and offspring of the men, with more than 1,300 men and women participating over the last seventy-five years.

They tracked health trajectories, marital success, career advancement, and other aspects of the participants' lives. They tested common assumptions about health and happiness, and the findings support some interesting conclusions.

More than money and more than fame, it is our relationships that are the stronger predictor of a happy life. Not only that, but strong relationships are a better predictor of future happiness and physical health, even when compared to social class, IQ, and genetics. The study even found that the strength of relationships of fifty-year-old men was a better predictor of future physical health than their cholesterol levels.

So what do we take from all this? The study shows that stronger relationships and broader relationship ties lead to greater levels of happiness. Bottom line: If you want to be happier, focus on your relationships.[6]

INDIFFERENCE

"Joy does not simply happen to us. We have to choose joy and keep choosing it every day."

HENRI NOUWEN

This enemy reminds me of one of my favorite comic strips from Bill Waterson's *Calvin and Hobbes*:

CALVIN AND HOBBES © 1993 Watterson.
Reprinted with permission of ANDREWS MCMEEL SYNDICATION. All rights reserved.

And there's the irony. Here we (and so many adults) are just as lost as a six-year-old boy when it comes to making sense of life. Which leads us to our next enemy: indifference.

Indifference can look very normal. You work, spend time with your family, watch some TV, hit the golf course every now and then. Nothing tragic there. That's because indifference comes from the inside. It's the person who says they just don't really care about the best way to live, something better to live for, or being happy.

Indifference can come from a lot of places.

Life can be hard. Bad things happen to people. The kinds of bad things we don't tell anyone else about. Things we carry around in the back of our minds in the darkness. The kinds of things we will never forget. Things we've done. Things that have been done to us.

Sometimes indifference prevents us from seeing our own value. Our self-worth gets so beaten down we don't think we deserve happiness or wholeness anymore.

Sometimes it prevents us from seeing a future. We feel like the past looms too large, or we fear it will repeat itself. Some of us don't think the future can be better than the past.

Sometimes indifference prevents us from feeling freedom. We can't escape what we've done or what was done to us. We feel like no matter what happens we will always be stuck in this place, stuck the way things are.

This is heavy stuff, but it's also reality. We don't like to talk about it, but no matter how good we are at ignoring the truth, it doesn't go away.

When we become indifferent, we are no longer seeking to thrive, but to merely survive. Just getting out of bed in the morning is the best we can manage. We search for a small slice of mediocrity to call our own, a comfortable hideout to protect us from the world. Then we stay there.

I wish we could escape these realities, but sometimes the only way out is through. There are no safe harbors to avoid life's storms.

Indifference wants to seem safe and comfortable, but it's a trap. It poses as a safe harbor but keeps us out in the storm.

Do the Fundamentally Happy experience life's storms? Absolutely. But they know of a force that is stronger than indifference. A force that serves as a lighthouse to carry them through the storm. Gratitude.

Gratitude and indifference can't coexist. The Fundamentally Happy are incredibly grateful. They recognize their blessings and keep a spirit of gratitude front and center in their hearts and minds. The storms rage, but gratitude carries them through.

One Fundamentally Happy person shared with me how he and his family cultivate gratitude in their hearts. Every night at dinner they say a quick prayer over their meal and then spend the next few minutes going around the table, one by one, listing off all the things they are grateful for.

He told me that their nightly gratitude list changed everything. If their kids were fighting, it made them stop and recalibrate. If he was carrying stress or anger from work home with him, it made him let it go. Even if he and his wife were in a terrible argument, it usually made them calm down and get perspective.

He told me that no matter what happens during the day, everything else washes away as he runs through the gratitude list with his family. A simple daily habit of gratitude changed everything.

When we are grateful, we want to pass on the blessings we have received. And that propels us forward.

Be grateful. Consider the blessings in your life. And don't start with the unique blessings; start with the monumental blessings: food, shelter, clothing, life, health, and so on.

When you cultivate gratitude in your heart, indifference will never find its way in again.

Neuroscience

YOUR BRAIN ON GRATITUDE

There is no doubt about it, being grateful and expressing gratitude is good for you. It is good for your physical and mental health, and it increases happiness and life satisfaction.[7] It is also good for your brain.

Showing gratitude increases activity in the hypothalamus.[8] The hypothalamus is the region of the brain responsible for regulating many functions, including eating, growth, metabolism, and sleep; it also regulates our reactions to stress. So it is easy to see how showing gratitude could impact your daily life.

For example, gratitude helps us fall asleep faster and stay asleep longer. And getting a good night's sleep can have a positive impact on many areas of our life. Gratitude can also relieve stress. Expressing gratitude has been shown to decrease levels of our main stress hormone, cortisol. Stress plays a role in depression. Therefore, it is not surprising that gratitude has also been shown to help reduce depression.[9]

Theory in Practice:
WHAT DO YOU REALLY WANT?

Want to see something fascinating? This is going to blow your mind.

Go ask someone this question: "If you could do anything, what would you do?"

You will be amazed at how many people can't give you an answer, or at best they give you an answer off the top of their head.

Or go ask, "What do you really want out of life?"

You'll get some vague answers, but it will be clear that the person has spent no serious time pondering the question. I can't decide if I'm more fascinated or saddened by how little time most people spend pondering what they want out of life.

Now ask yourself these questions. Take some time and think about them. Write down some answers on a postcard and keep it in your pocket or your wallet.

For one, you'll have a well-thought-out answer if someone ever asks you. But you'll also have a clear reminder of what you really want when the pull of lesser things starts to suck you in. Your answers can be as detailed or simple as you'd like as long as you take some time and really ponder your answer.

FEAR

"There is only one thing that makes a dream impossible to achieve: the fear of failure."
PAULO COELHO

A high school teacher was trying to teach her students about the compounding effects of bad choices.

She asked a young man to come to the front of the class and put his hands together like he was praying.

"Imagine you tell a little white lie to a friend," she said. She wrapped a piece of string around his hands and tied it.

"Try to break out of that lie," she told him. The young man snapped the string with ease.

"OK, let's try this." She asked the young man to put his hands back together.

"Imagine you tell a little lie to your parents, then you sneak out of the house and go to a party, and then you start drinking, and the next day you copy someone else's homework because you were up all night." She wrapped the string around the young man's hands again and again as the story got worse and worse. She brought up all the things that high school kids can get into: drinking, drugs, partying, lying, cheating, stealing, promiscuity, and so many other poor decisions.

By the time she was done, the boy's hands were wrapped in a thick layer of string.

"Try to break out of that," she told him. But even with his greatest effort, he couldn't budge. "The bad choices we make in life have a way of binding us. Small things bind us in small ways. Not many of the choices we make seem that bad when considered in isolation. But put them together, one on top of the other, and you will find yourself in a place much harder to escape."

The last enemy to our happiness is fear.

Living according to the Fundamental Theory of Happiness will require you to change the way you live. Not all of your thoughts, habits, and behaviors will align with the theory. If you want to be happy, some things will have to change. And just like the student in the story above, making one small change is as easy as snapping the string when it's wrapped around your hands once. But fear sets in when we think our whole life has to change. The decisions and habits we've built over years and years make it seem like we can never make the changes necessary to be Fundamentally Happy as the string wrapped itself again and again.

Sometimes we do things that contribute to our unhappiness and the unhappiness of others. Facing this truth can be painful, but our lives are our choices, and we are right where we are because we put ourselves here. That level of self-reflection isn't easy.

For some people, the Fundamental Theory of Happiness is a pivot, a slight turn in the trajectory of life. For these people, they might have to break through only a couple strands of string to pursue this new way of life.

For others, it might be more of a demolition project, tearing down the beliefs, systems, habits, and behaviors of the past and starting new. For this group, it might feel like that string is wrapped around your hands hundreds of times.

This fear manifests itself in a hundred different faces:

For some it's a fear of being alone—if you make the changes necessary, you'll end up losing or alienating friends or family.

For some it's a fear of consequences—if you face the mistakes of your past, you will have to pay the piper.

For some it's a fear of missing out—all that YOLO ("you only live once") malarkey.

For others it's a fear of failure—that old familiar foe that stops so many from doing what is possible and makes them settle for what is safe.

Fear of change—in all its faces—tempts us to rationalize with ourselves. *Life isn't that bad. It's easier to just go on as things are.* You might be tempted to give in to the fear that things can't get better and just give up on the pursuit.

How do the Fundamentally Happy combat fear? They dream.

This is not some "go for your dreams" cliché. I'm not telling you to shoot for the stars or to be all that you can be. The Fundamentally Happy have a firm conviction that the future can be bigger and better than the past. They have a firm conviction that what they have done and what has been done to them does not define them. So they dream.

They don't share the dreams of the world—like winning the lottery or owning a beach home. They dream of great relationships with their spouse and kids. They dream of financial peace and meaningful work. They dream of happiness, health, and vitality.

Dreaming gives them courage in the face of their enemies. It carries them to rise above the noise of the world and sustains them through the anxiety and resistance they sometimes feel.

Let yourself dream a little. Like a golfer who visualizes sinking his putt a thousand times before actually taking the stroke, imagine yourself discovering the lasting happiness we all yearn for.

In the end, you will either own the fear or the fear will own you. Which will you choose?

Hey, are you with me?

Write down five ways you or your life would change if you were really happy.

1. _____

2. _____

3. _____

4. _____

5. _____

THE LAST LESSON

"You have enemies? Good. That means you've stood up for something, sometime in your life."
WINSTON CHURCHILL

Your enemies are not stronger than you.

The forces that work against your happiness are not stronger than you.

I know these enemies well. I've experienced them. I've worked with thousands of people who have experienced them too. The Fundamentally Happy experience them.

This is the last lesson about your enemies: They don't go away.

You will always be tempted to choose things that are beneath you. You will always experience influences in your life that work against you and your happiness. You will always have to battle against the indifference and fear that make you want to settle for mediocrity.

But now you have the weapons to face your enemies—habits, awareness and filtering, gratitude, and dreaming. These are useful tactics if you choose to employ them. In fact, if all you implement from this whole book are these four tactics, your life will still change for the better.

Now we know our enemies, but the story isn't over.

Step IV:
The Permanent Principle

I WAS BORN FOR THIS

"Before I can tell my life what I want to do with it, I must listen to my life telling me who I am."

PARKER J. PALMER

My head was stuck in a shirt the first time she said it.

"What did you say?" I yanked my head through the shirt as my wife's voice came floating back.

"The stick turned blue!"

A pregnancy test is the most life-changing bathroom break you will ever take. I didn't know it was possible to hold that much fear and that much excitement in your heart at the same time.

We were having a baby.

We were both twenty-three, newlyweds, at our first jobs, and had just bought a house. Now a baby was on the way.

We discovered amazing things during that pregnancy. I'll never forget the first time I heard my baby's heartbeat. I could have listened to that quick and rhythmic thumping for days. I also learned about pregnancy cravings. I never knew one person could eat that much broccoli cheese soup and Caesar salad. And then there's that intertwining feeling of anticipation and excitement that seems to make every moment glow.

Of course, there are obvious reasons why that time is very different for a husband than it is for a wife, but there was one I never would have expected.

The second that strip turned blue, my wife became a mother. She had this immediate emotional and physical connection to our baby growing inside her. It was different for me.

I was excited and nervous, but I didn't feel like a dad. I did all the dad stuff. I painted the nursery and put together the crib. I figured out how to install the car seat and assembled swings and Pack 'n Plays and everything else. I loved doing it. But I didn't know what it meant to be a father.

After nine months of planning, prepping, and nesting, my wife woke me up in the middle of the night.

> "Don't get alarmed. I just want to let you know that I'm in labor. It's not time to go to the hospital yet, so you can go back to sleep."

I was not able to fall back to sleep.

By 6:00 AM we were driving to the hospital, and at 4:49 PM the nurse handed me the crying, slimy human being that was my son.

I looked at that face, and everything changed. I cradled my son in my arms and stared at him.

"My son. I love you so much. I love you unconditionally. I'd do anything for you. I will help you overcome any obstacle. I'll give you any good thing you need. I'll forgive you anything you ever do wrong. I love you so much I would die for you."

I didn't know much, but I knew one thing. I was a dad. I was born for this. I was born to be a father.

And in that moment, I felt more alive than I ever had before.

Hey, are you with me?

Have you ever had a moment of undeniable clarity? A moment where you absolutely knew something about yourself or the world around you was true?

Write down three things you absolutely know are true:

1. _____

2. _____

3. _____

SOME THINGS NEVER CHANGE

"I don't think life is absurd. I think we are all here for a huge purpose. I think we shrink from the immensity of the purpose we are here for."

NORMAN MAILER

Most people want to know who they are and what they are born to do, but the Fundamentally Happy obsess over a better question: What was I made for?

The problem is figuring out the answer.

The second I held my son in my arms, I knew I was made to be a dad. I wasn't ready for it, I hadn't learned it, I hadn't expected it, but I knew it. This gave me three important clues in my pursuit of happiness. Like a giant X on the map, it told me where to dig.

I call the first clue the Permanent Principle. The Permanent Principle is this: Any aspect of your life is related to your purpose in direct proportion to its permanence.

Let me say that again because it's that important: Any aspect of your life is related to your purpose in direct proportion to its permanence.

The more permanent it is, the more directly it is related to your purpose.

So much of life is in constant flux. I could look to my job for my purpose, but what if I get laid off? I could look to my hobbies or the sports teams I follow, but what if I move or I become interested in new things? I could look at my talents or abilities, but what if they change or become irrelevant? These things are fleeting. Work comes and goes, our abilities and talents wane, and our hobbies and interests grow old.

But not my fatherhood. That was permanent. This relationship wasn't going anywhere. It was a realization that opened the floodgates in my discovery of purpose and became one of my biggest clues into the lives of the Fundamentally Happy.

Enter the second clue: Even after I die, I will still be my son's father. That role—that relationship—is permanent even beyond my death.

From here I knew to look at relationships. So many of our roles and relationships change over time, but some do not. For example, I will always be a son. I will always be a father.

I will always be a brother. Not even death can erase those relationships.

It should be noted that the quality of these relationships changes with time and circumstance. Some people have a terrible relationship with their father, some don't. Some marriages end in divorce. But all of these relationships leave an indelible mark on us.

I was made to be a husband, a father, a brother, a son, and a friend. These relationships are more permanent than my own life and tell me more about my purpose than I could discover without them.

The third clue came late one night, and it hit hard.

I sat rocking my son back to sleep and began to wonder about his future. Like all parents, I have incredible hopes and dreams for my children's futures. And I began to wonder about my son's search for happiness.

I began to imagine my son asking the questions I was exploring. Would he find the answers I was searching for? What if he asked me, "Dad, what was I made for?"

Finally, the last piece of the puzzle clicked into place.

I would never be able to answer that question for him because I didn't make him. Sure, I'd made him in a physical sense, but that's cause and effect, and I was dealing at the level of purpose. He could ask, but truthfully, I didn't make him for anything. I didn't make his purpose.

A Fundamental Truth:
If I was made for a purpose, I must be made by
someone for that purpose.

My purpose didn't lie with my parents, who made me physically. It lay with my Creator, who made me purposefully.

Theory in Practice: THE PERMANENT PRINCIPLE

Apply the Permanent Principle to your own life.

1. Write down your different relationships: daughter, sister, mother, friend, coworker, acquaintance, and so on. _____

   _____

   _____

2. Rate your relationships from permanent to transient on a scale from 1 to 4 (1 is fleeting, 4 is unchanging). _____

   _____

3. Write down what that role means to you and your life. (For example, what does it mean to be a sister? A friend? A daughter? A mother?)

   _____

4. Rank your list from most important to least important. Use your gut. (For example, you would probably rank being a loving mother higher than being a trustworthy friend.) _____

   _____

   _____

5. Take a look at your list and read it in order. What does this list tell you about who you were made to be? _____

   _____

   _____

THE PRIMARY RELATIONSHIP

*"'I am [in your world],' said Aslan. 'But there
I have another name. You must learn to know me
by that name. This was the very reason why you
were brought to Narnia, that by knowing me here
for a little, you may know me better there.'"*

C.S. LEWIS, *THE VOYAGE OF THE DAWN TREADER*

I grew up spending significant time in both the Catholic and Lutheran Faiths. I even went to a Lutheran grade school and a Catholic high school. So it's safe to say that people have been telling me about God my entire life.

People always told me how much God loved me, but that never really meant much to me. I mean, of course God loved me. He's God! It's kind of his job.

I wasn't the most religious kid. If asked, I'd say I believed in God, but being Christian was little more than a name tag on my soul.

To be honest, I never really got it.

So when some friends invited me on a retreat my sophomore year of high school, I definitely didn't go because of God. But it was on that retreat I discovered why God didn't mean much to me.

I didn't know him.

I knew a lot about him. I had taken religion tests, read Scripture, and gone to Mass. I'd been told about God my whole life.

A Fundamental Truth:
*There is a big difference between knowing a lot
about God and actually knowing him.*

But God was still a stranger to me.

On that retreat I stopped simply knowing a lot about God. I met him. God wasn't just some benevolent being obligated to love me. He wasn't some distant force who put the world in motion and slipped away into the cosmos. God came close. I encountered him. For the first time I knew God loved me not because I was being told he did, but because I experienced his love. I knew he liked me. I came to know what he was like.

And I wanted to know him more.

I know people who think they dislike God, but they've never actually met him. I also know people who have been faithfully practicing their religion for decades without ever having really met God either. And I know so many people like I was back then, indifferent to God because they've never really met him.

Knowing God rather than knowing about God is incredibly important. You can't trust someone you don't know. If you really needed advice, would you go to a stranger? No. You'd go to a trusted mentor or advisor.

If you don't meet God, you can't know him. If you don't know him, you can't trust him. If you don't trust him, you won't ask why he created you. If you don't ask why he created you, you'll never know your purpose. If you don't know your purpose, you'll never really be happy.

The Permanent Principle is a compass. It always points toward our true north: our purpose. The Fundamentally Happy follow that compass, and it always leads to the same place. Our Creator.

Hey, are you with me?

Circle the number that best reflects how well you know God.

(1 being "not at all" and 10 being "perfectly or entirely")

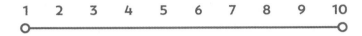

Circle the number that best reflects how much you trust God.

Now ...
Circle the number that best reflects how much God knows you.

Circle the number that best reflects how much God loves you.

A DANGEROUS ASSUMPTION

"If you want to identify me, ask me not where I live, or what I like to eat, or how I comb my hair, but ask me what I am living for, in detail, ask me what I think is keeping me from living fully for the thing I want to live for."

THOMAS MERTON

My pursuit of happiness led me back to that retreat when I was fifteen and pointed me to my Creator. So I asked the obvious question:

"OK, God, if you created me, what was I made for?"

I wore the sidewalks of my neighborhood down to gravel pondering this question. It turned over and over in my head in a hundred different forms:

Why did you create me?

What did you create me for?

What am I supposed to do?

Why am I here?

What am I made for?

I would ask the question during prayer after my kids went to bed. It would be lurking in the back of my mind during meals. I'd catch myself distracted by it at work.

One day I was out to lunch with a friend of mine, let's call him John, who is one of the Fundamentally Happy. John has raised beautiful sons and daughters who are happy, healthy, and holy. He's the kind of guy who, despite being an incredibly successful businessman, still drives a used car.

I told him about my journey and the questions that were racing through my mind. He told me this story:

John's family had gathered at his house for Thanksgiving dinner years ago. It was a day of great food, sharing stories, playing football in the backyard, and laughter.

As John was putting his son to bed that night, he asked, "Dad, why did you have me?"

A little confused, John asked, "What do you mean?"

"Aunt Karen was talking to Grandma about how happy she is that she doesn't have kids because it means she can do whatever she wants."

Karen is John's sister. She's a little older than John and has been married longer, but she and her husband never had children. They always said they would get around to it when the time was right. John's son didn't know that. He just knew that she didn't have kids.

"Dad, do you wish you didn't have me?"

John leaned over, put his son's face in his hands, and stared him directly in the eyes. "Never. You and your brothers and sisters are the best thing that has ever or will ever happen to me. Don't ever doubt that."

"But I don't do anything for you or mom."

"Son, your mom and I didn't have you so that you'd do something for us. We love each other so much that our hearts can't even contain it. You were born out of that love. You were born to be loved by us!"

After telling this story, John stared me in the eyes. "You keep asking God what you were made for, and you assume the answer to that question is something you are supposed to do. But I don't think we were made to do. I think we were made to be."

As I was driving home after lunch, I had to pull over. I kept rolling the story around in my mind.

John didn't have his son to do something; he had his son to love him.

I didn't have my sons so that they would do something; I had them to love them.

If that's true for my children, could it be true for me?

As soon as I asked the question, I knew it was.

God didn't make me to do something. He made me to be someone. God made me to be his child, to be loved by him and to love him back.

This was it.

MAKING SENSE

> *"You were made by God and for God and until you understand that, life will never make sense."*
>
> RICK WARREN

Sometimes it's hard to make sense of life. Truth doesn't always feel right, and lies don't always feel wrong.

But every now and then, a truth is revealed like the sun breaking through the clouds. You feel the warmth. You see the light. Everything finally makes sense.

Sitting on the side of the road alone in my car after that lunch with John, it was like the truth in my search for happiness had finally broken through the clouds. I knew it was true. I could feel it. Truth had come out into the light.

I wasn't made to do something; I was made to be someone. I am God's beloved son. I was made to be loved by him and to love him.

I began to test this truth from every angle. For the first time, I could see clearly. I knew where I'd gone wrong.

I had spent my whole life looking for one big thing I was supposed to do. Now I could see life wasn't about figuring out that one big thing. Life was about knowing that everything I did—big or little—either affirmed who I was or denied it. My whole life made sense in relation to this one simple idea.

This was it. This was the simple truth that drove the Fundamentally Happy. It wasn't about being rich or poor, healthy or sick, feeling good or feeling bad, being comfortable or uncomfortable, being praised or being scorned.

The Fundamentally Happy aren't trying to do or to have, they are trying to be. This simple truth is why the Fundamentally Happy can be found anywhere, in any state, and from any walk of life.

A Fundamental Truth:
You can have nothing but still have everything if you are living as who you are meant to be.
You can have everything but still have nothing if you are not living as who you are meant to be.

In everything—the big things and the small—you can be yourself, or you can be a shadow. Every thought, word, action, decision, or habit can either affirm that you are a beloved child of God, or it can deny it. Every thought, word, action, decision, or habit can either affirm that you love him back, or it can deny it.

Everything only makes sense in relation to this one simple idea.

Theory in Practice:
BEING VERSUS DOING

What we do doesn't inform who we are. Who we are informs what we do.

Find a blank hour-by-hour schedule and consider the last twenty-four hours.

Fill out your schedule hour-by-hour. What did you do? Who did you talk to? Where did you go? Be as specific as possible.

Once your recap is complete, go back and consider what really felt true to who you are. Put a star next to those times or activities. This could be something like working out, spending time in prayer, hanging out with friends, or playing with your kids. It could even be an hour at work where you were especially focused and devoted to what you were doing.

In the end, you'll have a clearer picture of which daily activities and interactions reflect who you are, and which activities or interactions fall short.

Step V:
The Elusive Art of Being

YOU'RE KILLING YOURSELF

"I think I began learning long ago that those who are happiest are those who do the most for others."

BOOKER T. WASHINGTON

David was seventeen and had just quit the varsity baseball team.

Everyone thought he quit because he was in band and couldn't handle the two commitments, but he didn't quit baseball because he loved playing guitar. What a silly idea. He could both pitch and play guitar if he wanted to. But these days David didn't want to pitch or play guitar.

He wanted to read.

As soon as school let out every day, David would get in his battered car—a white two-door that had been his dad's, then his older sister's, then his older brother's—and he would drive to the hospital.

And every day he'd head up to room 427, Anna's room. Anna was David's eight-year-old sister, and she was sick. In fact, she was dying.

Six months earlier, Anna had been diagnosed with the most curable form of children's leukemia. The diagnosis was a shock, but after that wore off, it felt like they had gotten lucky. A couple years of treatments and procedures, and then ten years from now this would just be a blip on the radar of her otherwise normal life.

But six months into treatment they discovered there was not going to be that normal life. This was no normal leukemia. Anna's leukemia was aggressive. Far more aggressive than her pediatric oncologists had seen before. The treatments were working, but the cancer kept coming back, and coming back more aggressive.

David watched all of this as he started his junior year of high school, and it all felt so surreal. David played on the varsity football team that fall, but by November his heart wasn't in it. He worked hard at his studies because that was his job, but all he really wanted to do was spend time with Anna. And Anna's favorite thing—ever since she had been a toddler and David a preteen—was for David to read to her.

David stopped playing sports and working his after-school job and most of his extra-curriculars. He just went to the hospital and read to Anna. For hours he would spend time with her, eat dinner with her, be there when other family visited. David never wanted to leave.

Seven days a week he spent at least five hours a day at the hospital. All the doctors and nurses knew him by name. He was even allowed special times to be with Anna beyond normal visiting hours because he spent so much time there.

One night, after reading to Anna until she fell asleep, one of the regular nurses caught David as he was leaving the hospital to go home that night.

> "Honey," the nurse said, "why don't you take a night off and go be with your friends. You're killing yourself coming every day like this."

> David's response: "For her I do it gladly."

David kept coming. Anna kept getting sicker.

She passed away before he began his senior year.

By the time David told me about Anna, he had three children of his own. She had been dead nearly fifteen years, but the lesson she taught David drove his life. He was one of the Fundamentally Happy who helped shape this book, and the lesson Anna had taught him was clear:

For love you'll pay any price. Even if it means killing yourself.

THE ATTACK ON LOVE

"It does not matter how long you live,
but how well you do it."

MARTIN LUTHER KING JR.

How far would you go for the people you love? Would you be uncomfortable? Would you endure pain? Would you die?

How better off would humanity be if everyone loved like that?

Or better yet, how better off would humanity be if everyone loved like you do?

Our culture waves the banner of love as an ideal, but in truth love has been diminished in three specific ways over the last fifty years. But our culture's version of love doesn't entrap the Fundamentally Happy. The Fundamentally Happy are free from the influence of the culture. And what are they most free to do? Love.

If you wish to be free like the Fundamentally Happy, you have to live and love counter-culturally.

Here are three ways our culture has diminished our freedom to love:

1. Love is diminished by language.

How many times have you heard someone say they love a restaurant, or they love their new smartphone, or they love a sports team? What do they really mean when they say "love"?

"This food makes me feel good."

"This possession gives me comfort."

"This team provides me with entertainment."

You might be tempted to think this is harmless semantics, but hear me out.

Throwing around the word "love" turns life upside down. It makes the important things trivial and the trivial things important. When we use the word love instead of what we really mean—"I feel good," "I'm comfortable," or "I'm entertained"—it reinforces false ideas about what love is. It prevents our understanding of real love.

2. Love is diminished through fantasy.

The ability to see things as they really are is one of the great life skills, but our culture has made it very difficult to see love as it is.

Fantasies are all over the place when it comes to love. The two extremes are the Disney dream and pornography.

On the Disney side, we have an idealized notion that love is about birds, rainbows, and singing farm animals. Love is pure emotion. It is an overwhelming feeling of infatuation and delirious joy. If you defeat the evil witch, you will have your happily ever after.

On the other side is the fantasy world of pornography, where love is pleasure and getting what we want. Men and women are objects we use to get what we want when we want it. It turns love into sex, and it turns sex into something selfish and dangerous.

3. Love is diminished through starvation.

In a speed- and size-obsessed culture—one that screams for every moment of time, energy, and focus—those we love are left starving for a kind word, a moment of attention, the smallest gesture.

We need to feed love with our time, energy, and attention. Love is a choice that is lived out through our kind words, simple deeds, meaningful tokens, and our very presence. When we give everything we have to the demands of the world, we are left starving and selfish. When those we turn to for love have given everything they have to the world, we are all left in a starving and selfish place.

The Fundamentally Happy I have interviewed for the purpose of researching this book, as well as the Fundamentally Happy mentors who have formed who I am today, aren't just aware of the ways our culture diminishes love, they intentionally rebel against it.

Does it take time to break free from the mindless routines of behavior and speech that conform us to the culture? Absolutely. Does it take practice to resist the fantasies our culture creates about love? You bet. Does it take incredible intentionality to save our very best for the people we love? No doubt.

But love is about freedom, and if you aren't free to love, you don't have much freedom at all. The time, practice, and discipline are worth it. Do you really want to live in a world where love is so diminished? If so, you need to ask yourself why.

Don't rush the process of decentralizing the culture's influence on you. It takes time. Soon you will see culture's grip loosen and begin to fail as you enter into a new freedom. A freedom where love can become the powerful force for good it was always meant to be.

Hey, are you with me?

Take some time and observe yourself. Make yourself into a case study in love.

How often do you say "love" when you mean you are comfortable, you feel good, or you are entertained?

How often do you fall into the trap of fantasy?

How often do you allow the time-famine, materialistic, and impulse-driven culture to starve those in your life from feeling your love?

A COMPLEX ART

"Luv Is a Verb."

DC TALK

Love is an art. It's as simple as a meaningful touch or making the bed without being asked. It's time alone and away from the noise of the world. It's a thoughtful gift or a kind word. It's all this and so much more.

But love is also complex. There is no magical or scientific formula to love. There are no love potions. No certain amount of inputs will yield the output of love. I can't give you a step-by-step guide that will help you be better at love.

Love isn't about something you do, and yet what other evidence can you show for your love than what you do? Sometimes we have to do something that the one we love does not want us to do because we love them. Other times the way we try to show someone we love them doesn't make them feel loved. And sometimes we can't do something the one we love wants us to do because we love them. It's confusing. Love is confusing. It makes my head spin just trying to type it all.

Take this example.

I love my wife and children more than anything in the world. I go to work because I am their sole financial support and I want them to have safety and security, food, clothing, shelter, education, and so many other things. I go to work as an act of love.

But every single morning, my children beg me not to go to work. Sometimes they even cry. Should I quit my job and stay home with them? If I didn't go to work, I could undoubtedly spend more quality time with them. I could give them what they wish! But what happens when the food runs out, or the mortgage can't be paid, or the tuition bill comes in?

Despite how much they beg me not to, I go to work every day because I love them.

So what do we do? That's exactly what I asked the Fundamentally Happy.

To be honest, every person I asked gave me a different answer:

- Never miss a game or recital. It's what your kids will remember most when they are older.

- As long as you're doing the best you can, your spouse and children will know and forgive any mistakes you make.

- Lean on and trust your spouse. Just as you can guide and lead, your spouse can guide and lead when you're not sure what you're doing is best for the love of your family.

- Never make a change only because it will earn more money. (In that person's experience, those were the worst decisions he has ever made.)

These are just a few examples, and they're all out of context of a longer and larger conversation, but I was looking for the common threads throughout their stories and wisdom. This chapter is my attempt to codify their responses.

A Fundamental Truth:
Love is an art. We show our love through what we do.

The model for loving like the Fundamentally Happy is built on three essential elements to a healthy and balanced approach to love. Consider them like the legs on a three-legged stool. A three-legged stool will never wobble, but if you take one leg away, the whole thing will come crashing down.

The three legs are loving yourself, loving others, and loving God. For each leg there is a set of specific and simple rules we can follow that will help us cut through complexity and live a life of love.

Theory in Practice:
ROLE MODELS AND MENTORS

I've always looked for great mentors. I learned early in life that experience is the best teacher, but it can sometimes be a brutal teacher. I'm always hoping to learn from the experiences of others.

Take some time and look for some mentors in your life.

Who do you know who is really good at love—loving themselves, loving others, or loving God?

Who seems like they have life figured out?

Who do you admire?

Who has a similar state in life as you, but is just a little further along the road?

Who do you look up to?

Get some blank sheets of paper. Write these people's names down, two on each page. One name at the top, the other halfway down. Start with the first name on the first page and set a three-minute timer.

Spend these three minutes writing furiously. Write characteristics, achievements, habits, and other qualities you admire in that person. When the timer goes off, move on to the next name and do it all over again.

This exercise will vary in length depending on how many names you start with, but in the end, you will have an incredible list. Spend time poring over your list looking for common themes and qualities.

This list won't just tell you a lot about these people, it will reveal a lot about yourself.

You can use this list in a few ways:

1) to help paint the picture of who you want to become,

2) to help you find intentional mentors who can speak into your life,

3) to help you see if you overvalue certain achievements or qualities or undervalue others.

If you need clarity on who you aspire to be, look no further than the people you admire.

IT STARTS WITH YOU

"A purpose of human life, no matter who is controlling it, is to love whoever is around to be loved."

KURT VONNEGUT

The Fundamentally Happy are good at loving themselves.

They're not self-centered. They don't think they are better than anyone else. They don't put themselves above others. But they do know how to love themselves so they can better love others.

The Fundamentally Happy father knows that he needs to exercise and eat right so he can walk his daughter down the aisle at her wedding. The Fundamentally Happy mother knows she needs a night every now and then to go to the coffee shop alone and read a good book so she can respond to the needs of her young family. The Fundamentally Happy college student knows that the more he or she excels in his or her studies, the greater gift he or she will be to the world.

The idea of loving yourself might make you uneasy. Many of us are conditioned to think it's selfish to focus on our needs. Mothers are the worst at this. My wife is constantly pouring herself out for our family and struggles to rest, recharge, and fill up again.

Getting over this conditioning is the first and hardest step to loving yourself. I would like to invite and encourage you to take this first step. In fact, I'll give you more than an invitation. I give you permission. The rest is simple compared to this first step.

In Stephen Covey's classic *The 7 Habits of Highly Effective People*, he breaks human nature down into four dimensions: physical, spiritual, intellectual, and emotional.[10] The beauty of this model comes from the clarity of thought it gives to how we approach loving ourselves.

If I asked you how you could best love yourself, you might have difficulty answering the question. It's too vague. But if we break our lives down into these four aspects, it becomes clear, and the question becomes easier to answer.

How could you love yourself physically?

- Eat healthy food.
- Exercise regularly.
- Get a full night's sleep.

How could you love yourself spiritually?

- Spend time in daily prayer.
- Read Scripture.
- Serve the poor.

How could you love yourself intellectually?

- Read great literature.

- Learn a new language.

- Keep a daily journal.

How could you love yourself emotionally?

- Invest in solid friendships.

- Find a daily time for solitude and silence.

- Get out into nature.

I intentionally kept these suggestions fairly vague so you can personalize them. Eating healthy could mean a thousand different things to a thousand different people. For one person that might mean getting in a habit of drinking six to eight glasses of water throughout the day. For another person it might mean getting into a habit of eating an energizing breakfast every morning.

It isn't important for everyone to do the same thing. The secret is to use the four aspects to find something practical and meaningful for your life.

Hey, are you with me?

Give yourself a letter grade for each of the four aspects of your life:

S is for surviving. You are just getting by.

G is for growing. You are on the right track, but you know you have work to do.

T is for thriving. You have this aspect covered and just need to maintain what you are already doing.

Next, pick one of the aspects where you are surviving or growing and come up with a simple and achievable change you can commit to over the next week. Write it down and stick with it. _____

_____

_____

INVESTING YOUR THREE MOST IMPORTANT RESOURCES

"The key is not to prioritize what's on your schedule, but to schedule your priorities."

STEPHEN COVEY

Thanks to the Permanent Principle, the Fundamentally Happy know the importance of relationships in their lives. Our relationships outlast everything else, even our own life, so we have to get these right.

But relationships can be tricky.

There are three personal resources that matter to relationships: time, energy, and attention. The difficulty is that these are limited resources. How do we maintain healthy relationships with our spouse, children, friends, parents, siblings, coworkers, neighbors, and countless other acquaintances that make up our relationship circle when we only have so much time, energy, and attention to give?

If I spend all of my energy and attention at work and save nothing for my wife and children, my relationships will be out of balance. If I do this day in and day out, it's likely that my relationships will suffer dramatically. But at the same time, I can't ignore my work. What do I do?

By the time I verified the outline of the Fundamental Theory of Happiness with the Fundamentally Happy, I knew I had already moved on to the question of how to live the theory. Good philosophy only gets you so far. I needed something I could act on. So I followed up with the Fundamentally Happy to see how they managed their relationships. I collected answers and insights and distilled them down into a basic structure for managing my relationships.

In essence, the Fundamentally Happy follow three simple steps to ensure thriving relationships.

1. Categorizing

The Fundamentally Happy get really clear about their relationships.

One Fundamentally Happy friend told me she only has time for one or two friends in her life. She knows some coworkers don't understand why she never accepts an invitation to hang out, but she has kids and a husband at home and very little time; she only has time for a couple of invested friendships. She doesn't let the lines get blurred.

I'm terrible at this. I have a tendency to blur the lines between coworkers, friends, and family, right on down the line. On that path, I rob from the relationships that matter the most to give to the relationships that matter the least.

The Fundamentally Happy are clear about their relationships. Now, don't confuse this with a cold dismissal or lack of care for people. The Fundamentally Happy are universally described as some of the most caring and generous people you would ever meet. But they also discern relationships and never let the lines get blurred.

This is especially important given the second step.

2. Prioritizing

The Fundamentally Happy prioritize their relationships using the Permanent Principle.

Basically, the Fundamentally Happy prioritize their relationships in terms of primary and secondary relationships.

Primary relationships are the relationships that cannot and do not change. Our relationships with our children, our spouse, our parents, and our siblings are a great start. Some friends will also fall into this category.

No matter what happens to me, I will always be a dad, husband, son, and brother. These relationships are permanent.

Two important things to note. First, when I say the relationships don't change, I don't mean the present emotional state of the relationship (do we like each other, have we connected, do we talk, and so on). Second, these relationships are not necessarily biological. For example, the relationship between a child and their adoptive parents would also fall into this category.

Secondary relationships are the relationships that can and do change. Our relationships with our friends, our work, coworkers, and neighbors are all secondary relationships.

Friends can fall into either category, but you have to be careful. We have a "culture of acquaintance" that we have turned into friendship, and the advent of social media and other non-traditional friendships can deteriorate the true meaning of this relationship.

The Fundamentally Happy don't get confused about which relationships are most important. They spend their personal resources on their primary relationships before their secondary relationships.

I asked one Fundamentally Happy mentor how he prioritized within the same relationship status. For example: How do you prioritize between your spouse and your kids, considering they are both primary relationships? His answer was brilliant.

He told me, "A thriving relationship between a husband and wife always reaps benefits for the relationship between the parent and child, but the same is not always true the other way. That's how you know your relationship with your spouse is a higher priority than your relationship with your kids."

A Fundamental Truth:
A healthy and thriving priority relationship always reaps benefits for a lesser priority relationship.

I learned a long time ago that brilliance was the ability to take something complex and make it simple, and in this moment, I knew this man was brilliant when it came to managing his relationships.

3. Invest

This is the last step the Fundamentally Happy use to manage their relationships.

The Fundamentally Happy don't spend their time, energy, and attention; they invest it.

Every use of time, energy, and attention given to a secondary relationship is at the service of a higher priority relationship.

Do the Fundamentally Happy work hard? Absolutely. Harder than most. But any late nights or extra hours are at the service of the benefit of their families. Do the Fundamentally Happy spend time with friends? Absolutely. The Fundamentally Happy have deep and satisfying friendships. They spend time with friends to recharge and stay emotionally healthy so they have more to give to their families. But the Fundamentally Happy never give any secondary relationship more than it needs.

Give someone your time, attention, and energy, and they will feel loved. That's not the hard part. Figuring out the right way to spend these resources is trickier. But these simple steps will help you invest in relationships that reap benefits in every aspect of your life.

Hey, are you with me?

Make a list of all the relationships you're currently in. Then work through categorizing and prioritizing them. If you are having trouble prioritizing them, remember the fundamental truth about relationships: A healthy and thriving priority relationship always reaps benefits for a lesser relationship.

YOU CAN'T EARN IT

"Grace means there is nothing we can do to make God love us more—no amount of spiritual calisthenics and renunciations, no amount of knowledge gained from seminaries and divinity schools, no amount of crusading on behalf of righteous causes. And grace means there is nothing we can do to make God love us less—no amount of racism or pride or pornography or adultery or even murder. Grace means that God already loves us as much as an infinite God can possibly love."

PHILIP YANCEY

Katie had a secret.

She was a straight A student, captain of the volleyball team, and led retreats for her youth group. She was kind to her siblings and always listened to her parents. Katie looked like the perfect high school girl.

But Katie's secret clawed at her from the inside. It was not something that she had done, or something that had been done to her. It was something she believed.

Katie believed she was worthless.

She tried to prove that belief wrong by achieving more and more, but it didn't help. She tried to pretend that everything was all right, but knowing that no one knew what she was really going through only made things worse. Every time someone told her she was smart or kind or had such a great life, she felt more and more like a lie. And she had been going on faking it for so long that eventually she felt like she was lying to the people she loved.

Thoughts of suicide came at times. At first it was nothing dramatic. Just an idea floating in her mind. She didn't dwell on it. But over time she began thinking of it more and more. Then she allowed herself to begin to wonder how she would do it.

Thank God she got help.

Katie brought her secret out into the light, and kind and gentle parents, friends, teachers, and counselors listened to her. They supported her. They helped.

As Katie shared her story with my youth group years later, she talked about how she viewed her life back then. She said she imagined a great human being assembly machine up in heaven that made all of us. "God would get up in the morning," she said, "flip on the machine, and people would start running off the assembly line down onto earth." Except she thought something went wrong when she came off the line. She felt like she was supposed to go into the reject pile. She felt like something was wrong with her.

She kept trying to earn God's love and the love of others by what she achieved. But the love and support of the many people who came to her in her greatest time of need and the presence of God in her darkest hours helped her know that she was loved. It wasn't because of what she did or didn't do. God loved her in her brokenness. God loved her in the darkness. Even there, he was with her. Why? Because she was loved for who she was, not for what she did. She had discovered the Fundamental Theory of Happiness, and it changed her life.

Why do I share this story now, when we are supposed to talk about how we love God? Because I think it's important to recognize that many people struggle with the idea that God loves them.

Some worry they aren't good enough. That God can't love them. That the things they've done and the things that have been done to them make them unlovable.

Others worry that God will only love them if they behave or think a certain way.

These are lies.

A Fundamental Truth:

It doesn't matter if you are the world's greatest sinner or the world's greatest saint; God loves you as much as he possibly could, and there is nothing we can do to make God love us any more or love us any less. The only thing we can change is how much we love God back.

The Fundamentally Happy don't try to get God to love them more. They try to show God through their thoughts, words, and deeds that they love him too. Why? Because of the fundamental truth from our last chapter: A healthy and thriving priority relationship always reaps benefits for a lesser priority relationship.

The Fundamentally Happy know there is no higher priority relationship in their lives than their relationship with God. They know that if this relationship is healthy and thriving, it will reap benefits for their relationship with their boss and coworkers, their relationship with their neighbors, their relationship with their husband or wife, and their relationship with their kids.

At the highest level, our relationship with God comes back to purpose. Living at the level of purpose, the Fundamentally Happy know that every single moment is an opportunity to affirm their purpose to be loved by God and to love him back, or to deny their purpose.

I'm going to share some of the habits the Fundamentally Happy form to make sure that their relationship with God is healthy and thriving. But a few points before we dive in:

One: I'm not covering everything you could do. I couldn't if I wanted to. This list is simple. Start here and you will figure out for yourself where to go next.

Two: This isn't a great spiritual discourse. I'm focusing on the "what" and hoping the "how" is self-evident. But the "why" is always most important. Why do we do these things? Because we love God.

Three: There is a danger that you could think loving God is transactional or legalistic. If I follow these few rules, I will earn my way into God's love. That's not the way God works. We can't reduce our relationship with God into a simple set of actions.

OK, here's the list.

1. Go to Mass every Sunday.

It's one hour every Sunday. Admission is free. You don't have to do anything but participate. It takes so little from us, but it's the foundation of what we can do to show God we love him.

Are we busy? Absolutely. Do we feel like going? Not always. Do factors like work and kids make this difficult? At times. But are any of these insurmountable obstacles? No. Find a church near you and go every Sunday.

2. Read your Bible daily.

Get a good Bible and start reading God's book.

Start with the first book in the New Testament: Matthew. Read a chapter a day until you make it through the four Gospels (Matthew, Mark, Luke, and John). These books share the story of Jesus' life.

Pick a time and place and do this every day. One chapter a day will take about ten minutes or less. Read through the four Gospels. Then do it again. Before long you will feel like you know God as a friend.

3. Practice a daily time of silence and solitude.

God wants to speak to you, but it can be hard to hear him. We live in a noisy world. Set a time and place to spend a few minutes each day in silence and solitude.

How long? Just three minutes. That's it. Start there and add to it over time if you wish. Pick a place that is comfortable and quiet and try to eliminate potential distractions as much as possible. Set a timer on your watch or phone and then be still for three minutes.

What do you do during these three minutes? Close your eyes and don't try to do anything. If your mind wanders, that's OK. In the eyes of the world, this should look like a total waste of time. Before long you will begin to feel comfortable in the silence. Soon after that, peaceful. Eventually you will yearn for that peace, and your prayer life will grow.

4. Give every day to God.

Every morning when you wake up, let your first actions and thoughts and words give the day to God. Change your alarm sound to something very specific that will remind you to do this (you could even record your own voice to tell you to do it).

As soon as the alarm goes off, get out of bed, kneel down, and say,

> "I am God's beloved child.
>
> My Father has a great plan for my life.
>
> God, I give my day to you."

Then get up and go about your business.

Go to Mass every Sunday, read the Bible for a few minutes each day, spend a few minutes in silence and solitude, and start every day by giving it over to God.

This list is too simple. It focuses on what to do but not why to do it. This list makes it seem like loving God is a simple set of rules to follow.

But we have to start somewhere. Take this list for what it is: a simple observation into the lives of some people who really seem like they know how to love God. It's a good place to start.

You may be tempted to move on to other things, thinking these are too simple. Remember that simple and effective do not mean easy. They are not as easy as they sound.

Our relationship with God is the relationship where we receive. God doesn't need much from you, but he has so much he wants to give you.

Hey, are you with me?

This chapter had four suggestions for your spiritual growth.

1) Go to Mass every Sunday.

When and where would you go to church?

_____

2) Read your Bible daily.

Do you have a Bible? Where is it? If not, make a note to get one this week.

3) Practice a daily time of silence and solitude.

Everyone is busy. You're going to have to make time for this one. When and where will you find silence and solitude?

_____

_____

4) Give every day to God.

Take out your phone right now and change your alarm tone to something different. This little change will remind you to make this offering every morning.

Neuroscience

RELIGIOUS SERVICES

Researchers from Duke University, Harvard University, and MIT conducted a research study with over 1,500 individuals attending services from twelve different religions. Their goal? To see if attending religious services would lead to greater happiness.

Many studies over the years have shown that large one-time boosts to happiness do not have the long-lasting effect that most people hope for. Why? Because we get used to being happy (see the Little Things study on page 48). In fact, studies show that the greatest chance for a single event to have a long-lasting impact on our happiness is if it is a negative event that decreases it.

The researchers wanted to see if creating small boosts of happiness over a long period of time could have the lasting impact on happiness that most people are looking for. They decided to look at attending religious services for their answer, assuming that attending religious services was something that many people do regularly and provides a positive boost to overall happiness.

They interviewed over 1,500 people from twelve different religions, and their assumptions were not wrong. Research proved that people did receive a boost of overall happiness from attending religious services. But there was more.

Not only does attending religious services increase happiness, regular and frequent attending of religious services correlated with increased overall happiness scores as compared to people who attended services but not as frequently. What does this all mean in laymen's terms?

The research showed that the more you attend church, the happier you will be.

The researchers wrote, "Improvement [in overall happiness] may not come from major events such as winning the lottery, despite the seemingly life-changing nature of such examples. Rather, it seems like the key for long lasting changes to wellbeing is to engage in activities that provide small and frequent boosts, which in the long run will lead to improved well-being, one small step at a time."[11]

WELLES REVISITED

*"The mystery of human existence lies not in just
staying alive, but in finding something to live for."*

FYODOR DOSTOYEVSKY

I never had the privilege of meeting Welles Remy Crowther, but I wish I had. His story is tragic but inspiring. He was too young to go. He was too good to go. I'm sure there are many people who would have taken his place so he could have stayed a while longer. Instead, Welles gave his life for dozens of people he barely knew.

I can't think of a better witness to the Fundamental Theory of Happiness.

Welles had everything the world told him would make him happy. He had a loving family, a great job, money, friends, health, and good looks. But Welles wasn't satisfied with the world's definition of happiness. He wouldn't be The Stranger in the Mirror. He wouldn't settle for The Man in the Mask. He knew something wasn't right, and he embraced his dissatisfaction. He leaned into it until he was ready to leave behind a prestigious career with a big paycheck to serve other people.

Welles didn't deal on the surface of life. He dove deep— infusing everyone he encountered with meaning and purpose. He left a lasting mark on all those who knew him. He turned to his dad as a trusted friend and mentor. His last call was to make sure his mom knew he was OK. And as to Welles' relationship with God, I will leave you with his dad's words, quoting from John 15:13: "Greater love has no man than this, that a man lay down his life for his friends."

Welles was a man of love. On a crisp and clear Tuesday morning, he put the good of dozens of strangers in front of his own life and, in the end, made the ultimate sacrifice. Welles could have saved two or three people that day, led a group down to the street, and rushed away to safety. He'd still have been a hero and he'd still be with us. But love compelled him to go back. Love compelled him to go further.

On that fateful morning many years ago, Welles gave his life as a shining example of what it means to live according to the Fundamental Theory of Happiness. He had been dissatisfied with the promises of this world. He had sought purpose and meaning for his life. He was a devoted son, brother, and friend. He was loved, and he loved. On that morning he gave everything he had for something greater than himself. And in those moments, he surely found the happiness that surpassed understanding.

Theory in Practice:
SACRIFICE

Most of us are not going to have to literally give our lives for someone else, but we are called to sacrifice for others. And sacrifice is hard. We need practice.

Make one small, but meaningful, sacrifice this week.

Here are some ideas:

Clean out your closet and leave only the things you actually like and wear regularly. Then take another two or three outfits and donate them to a local thrift store.

Make a significant donation to a cause you care about. By significant, I mean the kind of donation that hurts a little bit. Not so much that you can't pay the mortgage, but enough that you have to cut your number of coffee runs in half.

Find someone on the fringe of society—the homeless, the jobless, the uneducated—and offer to buy them coffee. Sit with them and ask about their story.

Offer to use your expertise for a cause that really needs it, for free.

Spend some free time volunteering at a local soup kitchen or homeless shelter.

The options here are endless. Use the list above or come up with something yourself. Doing something is more important than what you do. Just make sure it's meaningful.

ALWAYS REMEMBER

"So faith, hope, love abide, these three;
but the greatest of these is love."
1 CORINTHIANS 13:13

Who are you?

You are a beloved child of a loving God.

What are you made for?

To be loved by God and to love him back.

Don't forget it.

Part III:
The Last Things

HAPPINESS REVISITED

"There are no happy endings.
Endings are the saddest part,
So just give me a happy middle
And a very happy start."
SHEL SILVERSTEIN

Science will never make you happy. There is no A2 + B2 = Happiness. But if I had to whittle the Fundamental Theory of Happiness down to one sentence, it would be this:

A Fundamental Truth:
When you live like who you really are,
then you'll be happy.

If only that were as easy to do as it is to say.

The truth is, you are never done living who you were made to be. It is popular to say, "Happiness is not a destination. Happiness is a journey." In a sense, that's true. There is no "happily ever after." You'll never get to a point when you *achieve* your purpose. When you can say, "Great! I'm done now. Now I can move on to something else."

But in another sense, happiness is not a journey. The journey of life is not what we were made for. We were made to be with God. We won't really be happy until we are with him.

Every moment is a choice. Choose to live the Theory, to be who you were made to be and do what you were made to do. Or choose to be someone else and do something else. The choice is yours. But only one of those paths will lead to happiness.

The Fundamental Theory of Happiness won't take away pain or suffering, it won't make you feel great all the time, and it won't give you what the world says will make you happy.

The Fundamental Theory of Happiness is more like a winning strategy for a game of poker. You still have to play the game of life. You won't know what cards you'll be dealt, and you won't know what everyone else is holding. You'll be tempted to bluff and fake it. You'll feel high highs and low lows. Some days you will feel like you have the winning hand, to have the world just about wipe you out. But if you live by the Theory, you will be able to play and play well. Live and live well.

Happiness isn't something you have or something you do. Happiness isn't a feeling or a rush of emotion. Happiness is the peace and restful assurance that comes from living according to your purpose. When you are who you were made to be.

If you want to be happy in this life, just let yourself be loved by God and love him back. If you do that in this life, you will reach true happiness in the next. That's the secret of happiness.

Hey, are you with me?

Copy this in your own handwriting. Do it right now.
If you have an index card, write it on that and put it in
your purse or in your wallet. If you have a sticky note,
write it on that and stick it on the bathroom mirror. If
all you have right this moment is a gum wrapper, then
write it on that. It's important that you write it down.
Later you can rewrite it and stick it some place where
you'll be reminded over and over again.

I am a beloved son/daughter of God.
The whole point of my life is to let him love me
and to love him back.

THE FIVE MISTAKES

"Money can't buy happiness, but it can make you awfully
comfortable while you're being miserable."

CLARE BOOTHE LUCE

I hope you will soon be counted among the Fundamentally
Happy. A happiness deep in your soul. I hope you find a
happiness that surprises and infects everyone you meet.
A happiness that makes people want what you have. Live
according to the Fundamental Theory of Happiness, and you
will get there.

But you should know there are five common mistakes people
who know the Theory but remain fundamentally unhappy
fall into.

These five mistakes won't kill you, but they will derail your
pursuit of happiness. They seek to stop the train or pull us off
the tracks. You're better than that. They won't get you. You

aren't the type to go back. But it's always good to know what is working against you. Be ready so you can fight these mistakes off at their first attempt to steal your happiness.

1. Getting too busy

What is the easiest mask of unhappiness? Busy-ness. That's why so many people seem so busy. The busy person isn't happy or unhappy. They're just busy.

Now that you know the process, you also know that it takes work to implement. It's hard work. Becoming dissatisfied, living at the level of purpose, facing your enemies, applying the Permanent Principle, and practicing the art of being. What's easier? Being too busy.

2. Failing to put in the work

An idea is only as valuable as the action it inspires. Knowing the Theory isn't enough; you have to do something with it.

You have years of unhappiness ingrained in you. It's going to take work to get rid of that training. But over time you will develop new habits and it will get easier. It will be your new normal and won't feel like so much work.

3. Fantasizing about the past

Some of you might fall into this mistake simply because it is so darn sneaky. This culprit sneaks into our minds and whispers things like, "Don't you wish you could go back?"

We fantasize about what life could have been like. I struggle with this one. I catch myself daydreaming about what life could have been like had I only discovered the Fundamental Theory of Happiness earlier. The decisions I could have made. The mistakes I could have avoided. The changes that would have rippled through my life.

But the Fundamentally Happy do not live in the past. No amount of effort can change it, but we can change the future. The Fundamentally Happy are always focused on the now and the next. They don't get lost in the past.

4. Envy

Another dangerous pitfall. We become envious of others, particularly those who do not know the Fundamental Theory of Happiness.

It is easy to look at the lives of people who seem to have everything together by the standards of the world and believe they do not know the troubles you know. This is particularly true in our age of social media, when it is so easy to make life look so perfect.

Can we all agree to just stop that nonsense? No one makes it through life unscathed. No one. They have all the same demons as you and me (we probably have a few that they don't and they probably have a few that we don't). We all get some dings and scratches along the journey of life.

5. Going back to comfort

There is one thing the world has going for it. Comfort. Comfort won't lead you to happiness, but it sure can feel good.

This mistake has other names—laziness and procrastination are a couple. It is easier to be comfortable than to be happy. But you were made for more than comfort. Don't settle for it and don't fall into the mistake of comfort.

THE NUMBER ONE HAPPINESS HACK

*"The best way to cheer yourself up
is to try to cheer somebody else up."*

MARK TWAIN

I've said it over and over: This book isn't about philosophy. It's about strategy. An idea is only as valuable as the actions it inspires.

But the strategy takes time and effort to implement. Sometimes you just want a quick fix for those times when life stinks. Let's be honest. Life stinks sometimes. It just does. It doesn't matter what kind of strategy you have; sometimes you just won't feel good. You get sick. Your loved ones get sick. You lose your job. You suffer a loss or tragedy. You don't have enough money. You fight with your spouse. You can't find a spouse. Whatever it is, the cause doesn't matter. Sometimes we are just not going to *feel* good.

I'd like to give you a little hack to help you along the way. I've saved the number one happiness hack I know for last.

If you want to instantly propel yourself into *feeling* happy, then make someone else feel happy.

That's it. Easy and effective.

Need ideas?

- Go through the coffee shop drive through and pay for the person behind you.

- Give someone a meaningful compliment about their job performance.

- Hold the door open—for everyone.

- Buy someone a random gift.

- Send your mom a text message telling her why you love her so much.

- Call or send a letter or card to an elderly relative.

- Go to a nursing home and ask to visit with the patients who don't often get visitors.

- Buy a bunch of Pokémon cards and go to the children's hospital and give them away to kids.

- When at a restaurant or bar, look for an older couple on a date and secretly pay for their dinner.

- Go to a store you frequent and give the cashier a $5 gift card for a nearby coffee shop. They deserve it.

- Leave a RIDICULOUSLY large tip for your server.

These are just a few ideas. Come up with your own. Trust me, this is the number one happiness hack.

Theory in Practice:
SHARE THE BOOK

This book is not meant to end up on a shelf somewhere. It's meant to be lived.

It's meant to help people live a better life.

So if this book has helped you, help someone else by sharing it with them, be it sharing what you learned or gifting them a copy of it.

Bottom line, don't let this book die on a shelf somewhere. It must live through you.

THE LAST STORY

*"It is Jesus in fact that you seek when you dream
of happiness; he is waiting for you when nothing else
you find satisfies you; he is the beauty to which you are
so attracted; it is he who provokes you with that thirst
for fullness that will not let you settle for compromise;
it is he who urges you to shed the masks of a false life;
it is he who reads in your hearts your most genuine
choices, the choices that others try to stifle.*

*It is Jesus who stirs in you the desire to do something
great with your lives, the will to follow an ideal,
the refusal to allow yourselves to be grounded down
by mediocrity, the courage to commit yourselves
humbly and patiently to improving yourselves
and society, making the world more human
and more fraternal."*

ST. JOHN PAUL II, 15TH WORLD YOUTH DAY

I'm scrubbing my two-year-old's head, trying to keep the soap out of his eyes while the four-year-old splashes me with water. The eight-year-old is behind me brushing his teeth, and my wife is trying to change the six-month-old into pajamas. It's the middle of the bedtime routine.

I can feel the sweat droplets beginning to form on my brow as the two-year-old wriggles in my hands—then again, maybe it's just the splashing. From behind me my son asks, "Dad, if you had to choose between being happy and having a whole lot of money, which would you pick?"

Where did that question come from?

In one sense I have no idea. Maybe it was something his teacher asked him. Maybe a friend from school was talking about happiness with his parents and came up with the question. I'm fairly certain my son hadn't come up with it out of nowhere.

In another sense, I know exactly where it came from. Even at eight years old, we are still deeply concerned with happiness. Where is it going to come from? Where are we going to get it? What do we have to do to achieve it? How will I know when I see it? Can I buy it? Am I capable of it?

Be not concerned with pleasure, or power, or money, or fame. Be not concerned with accolades and accomplishments, achievements or status. Do not deal in commodities, material goods, human vanity, or beauty. You were made for more than that.

There is no greater human achievement than being exactly who you were made to be and doing exactly what you were made to do.

NOTES

1   Holly B. Shakya and Nicholas A. Christakis, "Association of Facebook Use with Compromised Well-Being: A Longitudinal Study," *American Journal of Epidemiology* 185.3 (February 1, 2017), 203-211.

2   Jennifer Aaker, Melanie Rudd, and Cassie Mogilner, "If Money Doesn't Make You Happy, Consider Time," *Journal of Consumer Psychology* (2011), papers.ssrn.com/, August 2019.

3   Charles Duhigg, *The Power of Habit: Why We Do What We Do in Life and Business* (New York: Random House, 2014), 19.

4   L. Sherman et al., "The Power of the Like in Adolescence: Effects of Peer Influence on Neural and Behavioral Responses to Social Media," *Psychological Science* 27.7 (2016), 1027-1035.

5   L. Sherman et al., "What the Brain 'Likes': Neural Correlates of Providing Feedback on Social Media," *Social Cognitive and Affective Neuroscience* 13.7 (2018), 699-707.

6   Robert J. Waldinger and Marc S. Schulz, "What's Love Got to Do with It?: Social Functioning, Perceived Health, and Daily Happiness in Married Octogenarians," *Psychology and Aging* 25.2 (June 2010), 422-431.

7   P.C. Watkins et al., "Gratitude and Happiness: Development of a Measure of Gratitude, and Relationships with Subjective Well-Being," *Social Behavior and Personality: An International Journal* 31.5 (2003), 431-452.

8   R. Zahn et al., "The Neural Basis of Human Social Values: Evidence from Functional MRI," *Cerebral Cortex* 19.2 (2008), 276-283.

9   M. Ng and W. Wong, "The Differential Effects of Gratitude and Sleep on Psychological Distress in Patients with Chronic Pain," *Journal of Health Psychology* 18.2 (2012), 263-271.

10   Stephen Covey, *The 7 Habits of Highly Effective People: Powerful Lessons in Personal Change* (New York: Simon & Schuster, 2004), 300.

11   Daniel Mochon, Michael I. Norton, and Dan Ariely, "Getting Off the Hedonic Treadmill, One Step at a Time: The Impact of Regular Religious Practice and Exercise on Well-Being," *Journal of Economic Psychology* 29 (2008), 632-642.

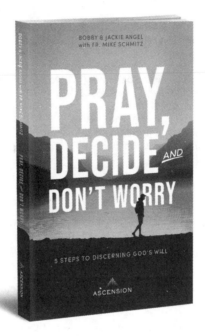